VOICES OF THE 21ST CENTURY

Women Who Influence, Inspire,
and Make a Difference

GAIL WATSON

MOJI
Keep sharing Your Truth —
You are making a difference.
Thanks for all you do!

WSA

PUBLISHING

Published by
WSA Publishing
301 E 57ᵗʰ Street, 4ᵗʰ fl
New York, NY 10022

Watson, Gail
     Voices of the 21ˢᵗ Century: Women Who Influence, Inspire and
     Make a Difference
     LCCN: 2018909397
     ISBN: 978-1-948181-19-8
eBook: 978-1-948181-20-4

Cover design by: Joe Potter
Copyediting: Claudia Volkman
Interior design: Claudia Volkman

www.womenspeakersassociation.com

DEDICATION

Dedicated to every woman.
May you use your voice to influence, inspire,
and make a bigger difference.

CONTENTS

AN INVITATION

Liora Mendeloff

> *Our vision is of a world in which women*
> *are empowered to authentically express themselves;*
> *to build a thriving, prosperous business;*
> *and feel a part of something greater.*
> *A world in which women take ownership of*
> *and step into being the leaders that they are;*
> *using their voice to powerfully inspire others,*
> *thus causing transformation in the lives of their clients,*
> *their companies, communities and the world.*
> —Women Speakers Association's Vision Statement

We are at a defining moment in history—a time when the world as we know it is transforming into something greater than we could ever imagine. We are moving out of a "survival-of-the-fittest" mindset, in which control, competition, and winning are king, and into a more level playing field, grounded in collaboration and contribution—one with women at the forefront . . . the leaders of the twenty-first century.

This new era requires us to shed our old skins, break through self-imposed limitations, and stretch beyond what feels safe, comfortable, or familiar. It's time for us to be gently honest with ourselves and invite our hearts to speak to us. It's time for us to move out of our heads and allow greater love and compassion to emerge—not just for ourselves, but for the greater whole. As we find unity between head and heart, we restore harmony within and also set the stage for humanity's great awakening.

It's time to fully be the creators that we are—to conceive new mindsets, new models, and new methodologies; to consciously design our destiny; and to lead by example for future generations to do the same. To accomplish this, we must be willing to come out of hiding, be vulnerable, and share our voices.

Many of us feel that speaking our truth is scary or even dangerous. Pain and suffering occurs in silence, though, and when we can find our voice, we experience a newfound freedom. Our voice is our soul's purpose activated, and no longer will it be suppressed. The deep wounds and trauma imprinted into our cellular memory from eras of atrocities endured by women, simply for expressing ourselves, are asking to be healed once and for all. It is time to move beyond the fear and speak up!

I don't say this lightly. I know this takes tremendous courage, which is why, as more of us rise up to use our voices to educate, guide, and inspire, we must support and empower one another to question everything, disrupt the status quo, and break new ground. *We* are the mapmakers. *We* are the trailblazers. *We* are the ones shaking things up and causing serious transformation on this planet.

But . . . we're not meant to do it alone.

It is time for our sisterhood to be a true sisterhood—a safe space for women to listen to one another without comparing, without judgment so we are empowered to reclaim our sovereignty and express our essential self.

We were all born with a seed planted in our heart. That seed is our essential self. We have been nurturing, feeding, and watering that seed with the wisdom and compassion acquired through the many hardships, heartbreaks, and challenges we've experienced on our life's journey. Now is the time for those seeds to at long last emerge, and for the radiant beings we are to be seen.

You came into this life with a message, a mission, a divine purpose. You have chosen to be here at this moment in time . . . right here, right now . . . to free yourself from the cycle of suppression, to be seen, to be heard, and to be acknowledged. Now more than ever, the world needs you! By reclaiming your voice and thereby breaking that cycle, you symbiotically empower all women to come out from behind the veil, reclaim their freedom, and become the sovereign beings they were born to be.

Your voice is your ticket to freedom—from abuse, from seclusion, from whatever has bound you or kept you silent.

There is no one right way or better way to express one's calling. One woman's message is not more significant because she has delivered it from the floor of the UN. There is no hierarchy when it comes to sharing our unique expression. So, remember . . . whether your stage is the classroom, the boardroom, or the kitchen table . . . your voice matters!

As you read the pages that follow, I invite you to stay in your heart and, without judgment, receive each message being shared. Remember that behind each story is a woman bold and brave enough to have her voice be heard. This isn't about perfection or even about being in agreement; it's about honoring each of our distinct voices and the journey that brought us to where we are today . . .

Voices of the 21st Century is a door opener, a conversation starter to stir the pot and invite you, the reader, to look within, listen to *your* soul's calling, restore harmony between head and heart, and set free your sovereign spirit.

Liora Mendeloff *co-founded Women Speakers Association (WSA) and served as its founding president from 2010–2014. Since completing her five-year tenure with WSA, she has continued to support its growth as a stakeholder and senior advisor. A passionate mapmaker and maverick at heart, Liora persists in shaking up the status quo, breaking new ground, and following her heart's calling . . . to honor the human spirit and all sentient beings, awaken humanity's memory of its divine sovereignty—thus, restoring heaven on earth.*

www.womenspeakersassociation.com

The Power of Community

Gail Watson

They say I'm part of the Sandwich Generation—a woman who is taking care of her kids and aging parents. Who knew it could be so destructive!

I was living a great life, no drama. I had been raised by parents who encouraged me and made me believe I could do anything I wanted to in this world. I was earning a large salary, feeling empowered and successful. While working in a fast-paced company that involved a great deal of travel, I was also managing my mother's Alzheimer's. Her illness had taken a sudden turn for the worse, and her behavior was becoming violent. My father, who was struggling to care for her, often called me in the middle of my workday, and I'd have to drop everything and go running. Very quickly things went downhill and I felt out of control. In May I was being celebrated as a top performer in my company, and ninety days later I was fired. I went from a hero to a zero.

I have described this time as being on a smooth flight when suddenly you hit turbulence that won't stop. This turbulence lasted close to twelve years. To the outside world, I kept smiling. I didn't ask for help, and like a bad cancer, the toxic energy of what was happening built up inside me. Eventually my body physically reacted to the stress inside of me. I started losing my hair, I couldn't sleep at night, and when I was lying in bed wide awake, I couldn't cry, but tears would dribble out of my eyes. I felt alone. Being fired was the biggest blow to my ego, and I never returned to the corporate world.

Soon after, I was introduced to the entrepreneurial world and found myself running a women's networking group. It was two years later that I reluctantly uttered the words "I was fired" when I was giving a speech. A reporter in my audience picked up on my story, and soon after there was an article in the paper with the headline "Fired for Caring." Now everyone knew, and my inner voice told me that I would lose all respect from my contacts in the corporate world, that I was not worthy of success, that I wasn't strong enough . . . that I was a failure.

1

I continued to be very involved in my mom's care, busy with my own young kids, and going broke because our second income was not there.

No matter what I seemed to do, I couldn't get unstuck from this place I was in. At the same time, even feeling like such a failure, often my friends would comment on how positive I was and how strong I was . . . What were they seeing that I wasn't?

It wasn't until I started to open up and share the truth of where I was that I started to receive help and answers. The entrepreneurial women in my networking group surrounded me with kindness and encouragement, and they made me believe in myself . . . again. They were rebuilding me with words. When I think back to my childhood, that's the foundation my parents built for me.

When the opportunity came to be a co-founder of Women Speakers Association, I made a personal vow that no woman's business would go down because "life happens."

What I've learned is that life does happen, and sometimes it serves up situations we feel we cannot handle—and sadly some of us don't. What I know, though, is that no matter how low we go, if we have a community, a network, some kind of support around us, we will not and cannot fail. It is crucial for you to be part of a network outside of your family or close friends—a group that you've connected with because you share similar likes or interests. This is a group that will know how to catch you when you fall.

I speak to hundreds of women every year—it's what fuels me. I love getting to know each and every new member who joins Women Speakers Association. When I hear they are stuck, when I sense they are feeling alone, when my heart aches for them, I let them know they are not alone. I make sure they know that they don't need to be alone, and that by surrounding themselves with a community of like-minded women, they will make it.

I have redefined success. I used to measure success by my earning power, but today I measure it by happiness. I receive and am filled with happiness when I am in service to others. The more I give, the more fulfilled I feel. Kindness changes everything.

How can we be kind? It's the small things. When in a conversation, ask questions and go a little deeper. Listen, really feel that person, and think about how you can help.

Smile! It might not come naturally when you're feeling a little low yourself, but that's the very time to consciously smile as you pass a stranger on the street or are next to another driver at a stoplight.

Words are powerful. Always use encouraging, positive words. Words are like fuel—and you never know when someone's tank is on empty. Your kind words might literally keep another person going.

I was down, I was broken, and no one knew because everyone saw me as the "strong one." It was the kind words of others that slowly brought me back and saved me.

Helping another person starts by taking action. It starts with each one of us taking responsibility and watching out for the individuals who cross our path, stepping away from our ego and giving others our attention, our kindness, and our smiles.

To the world, you might be one person, but to one person, you might be the world.

Gail Watson is president and founder of Women Speakers Association (WSA), the go-to place for innovative leaders, change-agents, and women with a message to connect, collaborate, and grow their visibility worldwide in order to fulfill their mission. As the first-ever global community for women speakers, WSA provides a platform for women to get seen, booked, and paid AND be part of a growing network reaching women in 120 countries.

www.womenspeakersassociation.com

THE DEFINING MOMENT

Saana Azzam

From 2010 to 2016, I was immersed in the competitive financial sector and believed I had everything figured out. Dubbed as one of the top performers worldwide, I was en route to a very successful banking career. I had many accomplishments, which included hitting record sales in the MENA region. During this time, I believed that I had achieved true happiness in my career—as if life couldn't possibly improve. Financially secure and content with my job, I continued on diligently without question.

One day, I began considering whether my successful career fulfilled my moral obligations. Writing down a list of my humanitarian values, I discovered there was a massive expanse between my values (who I wanted to be) and my role (who I currently was). Altruism? Honesty? Integrity? The realization that my career lacked some of these properties forced me to admit that a large part of me was unfulfilled with my chosen path. Despite the joy I felt in the financial sector, it was apparent that I couldn't continue knowing that I was not being true to myself or making a difference to others. After resigning almost immediately, I contemplated what I would do next. I knew unequivocally whatever it was had to be based on my values.

I decided to launch my own speakers agency. My goal was to set up a scalable social impact agency that focused on bettering others. I wished to empower and educate others—to lead them on a better journey rather than merely creating a company focused on generating immense amounts of capital. From this simple idea, MENA Speakers was born. I knew that setting up a speakers' bureau in this region would be challenging as this profession was unknown to a great majority of the people. For the first time in my life, I experienced the fear of failure.

My first big break came days after the launch of MENA Speakers when

I was asked to organize an important speaking engagement for a very special guest. The fact that I was completely inexperienced in this field left me feeling apprehensive and extremely nervous; I was faced with a challenge that could either make or break my career. The guest of honor was Thabo Mbeki, the second post-democratic president of South Africa. Not only was I tasked with my inaugural engagement as a newly launched public speaking agency, I was under pressure to organize an exclusive guest list and adhere to the wishes of many important people. Failure was not an option.

Despite my inexperience, I performed to the best of my ability. I constructed a VIP guest list comprised mostly of CEOs I had either met or read about. With local and foreign dignitaries in attendance, I felt extremely uneasy about my opening keynote. How could I possibly leave an elegant and lasting impression while satisfying the needs of my exclusive audience? On top of this, how was I supposed to honor His Excellency Thabo Mbeki without diminishing the importance of the prominent guests?

I rewrote my speech at least a dozen times to ensure it was as perfect as it could be, and I polished my public speaking skills to combat my nerves in anticipation of this crucial event. I found myself utilizing skills I previously had taught my clients—techniques to tackle my nerves, such as the NLP techniques of laughing or yawning to inhale oxygen and slow nerves. But nothing diminished the fact that my new business was riding upon this engagement.

On the day of the dinner, February 19, 2016, I prepared myself and conducted a final inspection to make sure everything was in order before making my way to the five-star hotel in Dubai. As I stood in front of everyone, with sweaty palms and a smile plastered on my face so forcefully that my cheeks hurt, I stared into the important faces in the audience. In that moment, I knew my life was about to change, and despite the nerves, I was ready to dive in head-on. I was ready to become the very best version of myself. Clearing my throat, I began the speech I had perfected.

My flawless deliverance and the success of the entire event lifted my spirits, and I regarded this as an omen that I was on the right path. The humility of my esteemed guests further filled me with great joy. I was finally fulfilled, and I knew this was what I was born to do. From that moment forth, the sacrifices were repaid in full as I came to the conclusion that seizing the opportunity for change—despite risking everything—was completely worth it.

In every person's life, there is a moment that causes you to question who you are and what your purpose is—a moment that defines you. When faced with this moment, do you risk everything and strive for greatness? Or are you content with the confines of mediocrity? If you choose to act with congruence, you'll experience true happiness and achieve your full potential. Seize your own defining moment!

Saana Azzam is the founder and managing director of the leading speaker's bureau in the Middle East, MENA Speakers. She represents over two hundred intellectual and impactful voices in the region. Dubbed the "experts' expert," Saana is skilled in the art of high-powered public speaking and communication and also coaches others in the art of giving memorable speeches.

www.mena-speakers.com

RAGING AGING

The #WeToo Movement

Renee Balcom

At fifty years old I had an awakening: I realized that I was aging. I even received an unsolicited AARP card that implied I was nearing retirement age. Wow! Then, when my eyes were opened, I realized that my entire peer group was also aging, including my husband and my best friend. In fact, we are all aging! So why is this such a negative event in our lives and in our culture? I must admit that I was a little freaked out by this awakening. After all, who among us really wants to get "old"? But there it was, staring me square in the face. . . . I have always been one to overcome my fear by intellectualizing it, breaking it down, and learning to understand what issues are causing me to be afraid. So I began a journey of discovery—and boy, were my eyes opened!

Life has a way of presenting us with what we focus on. Suddenly my life was filled with "older" people, people well into retirement (up into their nineties)—and for the first time I realized that they were having fun. Not all of them, of course, but most of them were living lives that were full, vibrant, and rich. I became more and more curious—where was this joy coming from? Didn't they realize they were old?

I want to introduce you to Jane. Jane is eighty-six years old, and she is amazing. She lives alone in a beautiful home that she shared with her husband for over sixty years. Jane is tall, slender, and magnificent. She loves fashion and keeps a very full social calendar. She goes to yoga classes three times a week, she volunteers with her church and her ladies' clubs, she plays bridge like a professional—and oh, did I mention that Jane is legally blind? She has severe macular degeneration, but nothing holds Jane back. She is confident and informed. She is vibrant and filled with a lot more life than her eighty-six years would suggest. And she is one of hundreds of aging adults I have met living similar lives. Jane is part of the Raging Aging movement. She and her peers are not taking aging lying down. They are committed to living full lives and are often heard saying that they "just don't feel old."

So here are the facts: 96 percent of Americans over the age of sixty-five live their lives independently. Forty-seven percent of those over age sixty-five still hold down jobs. Most have active sex lives, are avid sports fans, and participate fully in life. In fact, when I asked this group about their thoughts on aging, I received almost unanimous support for the wonderment . . . the joy of aging—the very thing so many of us fear.

I heard responses like, "Now I can make a difference"; "I live in the present"; "I know more about love than when I was younger"; and "When you are young, you are so busy doing that you forget to live—age teaches you to value life." I began to understand that, just like all times of our lives, aging is a mindset; we get to choose how we will age—just as we chose how we lived out our youth. Choices continue to be the dominate ingredient in the recipe of life that we create for ourselves.

My journey took me into a newfound paradigm, a place where there is a zeal for life and living. My encounters changed my eyesight, teaching me to see differently, more clearly. I don't feel sorry for "old people" anymore—I envy them. I know I saw the very face of God in the courage and enthusiasm of the people I met along the way. And now I look for that face every day, hoping to brush up against wisdom and love, bravery and the ability to persevere.

My friends, this is a Call to Action—our Manifesto. We are the baby boomer generation, the largest and most influential generation of people to exist in the world. We have created great change in all aspects of culture, and our impact on society has been felt for over seventy years. From political influence and economics to dance, music, and yes, technology, our generation has had the most influence on society to date. We are the authors of tolerance, acceptance, and diversity. And we control 77 percent of all American wealth. Yet we are facing a future of marginalization and discrimination if we don't effect change now and call for an end to ageism in our society. Ageism is the last acceptable form of discrimination in our culture.

We have the power in numbers and the wealth to demand that respect and dignity is provided to everyone in our communities. We should no longer tolerate the rampant discrimination toward us, the aging population, and instead we should celebrate longevity as they do in many other cultures. We need to put a stop to the exploitation that is focused on each one of us and instead demand that we are celebrated.

We are the #WeToo Movement.

We can change biases, but we must begin with ourselves. TODAY, starting NOW, change your point of view about who you are in your aging. Remind yourself that you are vital, magnificent, created with a plan and purpose. Your purpose doesn't end at a set time or age; it goes on as long as you are alive. Stop looking at yourself as aging and see yourself as the warrior you are. We will not go down in defeat; we will not allow ourselves to be housed or placed in positions of insignificance. Now take this newfound freedom and project it to your families, neighbors, and communities. It's time to stand up!

Webster defines *raging* as "intense enthusiasm, passion, a fit of wrath." Let's participate together in RAGING AGING. Let's stand together, protecting the frailest among us, and commit ourselves to age—with intense enthusiasm, passion, and in a fit of wrath.

*Advocate **Renee Balcom** is the founder of the Raging Aging #WETOO MOVEMENT. She is passionate about changing the cultural norms about aging. After working with hundreds of people who are classified as age-ed, Renee came to realize that most of the information being provided to us about aging is wrong, most of our beliefs about aging is wrong, and her mission is to set the record straight. Renee is frequently asked to speak about changing the cultural attitudes about aging.*

www.reneecompany.com

THE MAGIC OF A BOLD GOAL

Melanie Benson

What do you think you could achieve if you had the confidence to step into a more daring and bold version of yourself? An audacious goal? A bold vision? The ability to truly create a legacy and impact on this planet? The energy of a bold goal catapults you forward and ignites a more fulfilled and expansive you.

Maybe you have a mission that is so big you have no idea how to pull it off. A bold goal ignites your focus. Bold goals require you to become more resourceful, more confident, and more committed, ultimately challenging you to stretch beyond your comfort zone to become the person who can achieve any outcome.

If you have a bold goal in mind, you know what I mean. Your goal probably has been roaming around in your mind for some time now, evolving into something way bigger than you know how to pull off. It feels simultaneously inspiring and terrifying, but the thought of not pursuing the goal leaves you feeling unfulfilled. Yet you just can't get this idea into motion.

Maybe you can relate to one of these two scenarios:

1) **You are determined to conquer your bold goal, so you commit and jump in.** But you don't know what you're doing, so confusion kicks in. What steps should you take? You've never done this before, and you don't know anyone who has. Fears and doubts take over as you imagine all the ways this could become an epic fail. You could run out of money, perform miserably in front of your colleagues and friends, or ultimately lose everything you've worked so hard for. Now your previously inspired mind is in full-blown panic. Your logic mind chimes in, providing you with several rational and perfectly acceptable reasons that this idea is crazy. You decide to dump it and work on something more tangible and "safe."

2) **You find yourself in a state of limbo.** Your old goals no longer motivate you, and your thoughts are spinning as you try to find a new direction. You've pursued a few different paths, but nothing is

lighting your fire. Bored, frustrated, and a bit disillusioned, you feel disenchanted with no clear vision of what's next. If you are a high achiever by nature, you're miserable because you pride yourself as someone who's always in motion. If you are more of a "slow and steady" person, this lull has pretty much taken you out of the game. Being caught in ambiguity has slowed you down to a full stop.

The second scenario was my story. I found myself a few years ago in that state of limbo. Having accomplished great success, I had hit a wall of uncertainty. Not feeling particularly inspired by any new direction, I felt stuck. I knew I wasn't "done"—I just couldn't reignite my fire! Having overcome so many limitations, this stage was frustrating and demoralizing.

But then I set a really bold goal. Instead of just trying to find the next step, I went BIG. I set my sights on a level of success I had never achieved. Instead of falling back on old patterns, I had to awaken a new level of leadership. Connecting to a bold goal was my pivot point. I found opportunities rolling in faster than I could keep up while revenues began to multiply again.

Let's look at how the power of a bold goal can help you pivot and ignite new levels of success:

- A bold mindset dissolves fear and doubt that normally hold you back.
- The energy of a bold goal shakes away mental cobwebs for greater clarity.
- Confidence and courage soar through your body so you can take actions that you've been unwilling to take.
- Resources and million-dollar connections seem to magically appear.
- Influence, impact, and income expand exponentially with grace and ease.

Now, don't let one of the two biggest reasons smart, talented people fail to achieve their goals derail you! Here's what they are:

1) **"I Don't Have Time"**—Time can be your greatest enemy; most people fill their days with their current life priorities, ultimately believing they never have enough time to pursue anything else. But people who achieve their bold goals create time because their goal has become their priority.

2) **"I Don't Feel Capable"**—When you want to do something you've never done before, doubts often cloud your thinking and you can start to believe that you aren't capable. Perhaps you don't know where the money will come from. The gap starts to widen, and the mental trash kicks into high gear.

In his book *The Magic of Thinking Big*, Dr. David Schwartz says, "Belief, strong belief, triggers the mind to figure out ways and means how to." When you believe fully in your bold goal, you activate the most resourceful part of you. Resources that seemed blocked before will become obvious. Obstacles will no longer stop you as you will be determined to find a way, no matter what. Belief is part of the Bold Goal Formula that shatters your limits and kicks your motivation into high gear.

Isn't it time to shatter your limits and really start making the impact you dream of? Whether you are an influential leader already or you have a compelling mission to make a greater impact, using the Bold Goal Formula will serve you for a lifetime. Decide you will go for your bold goal. Commit to becoming the person who can pull it off!

Melanie Benson, *host of Own Your Bold Challenge, is a Success Amplifier. She hosts the* Amplify Your Success *podcast, is author of* Rewired for Wealth, *co-author of Entrepreneur.com's* Start Up Guide to Starting an Information Marketing Business, *and her success tips are featured in* Bloomberg Business Week, Woman's Day, *and* Parenting Magazine. *Melanie serves on the Women Speaker's Association Executive Team as well as the Association of Transformational Leaders. Growth resources are available on her website.*

www.melaniebenson.com

THE CIRCLE OF LIFE

Create the Radiant Life (and Death) You Desire

Dr. Janet Bieschke

We plan for the arrival of a new baby. We plan for the purchase of a new home. We strategize on how to move from one job to another to enhance our career. We may work with a financial planner to manage our savings and investments. And yet for the one most emotional situation in life—the one that affects the people who love us the most—many times we do absolutely nothing. We have no plan for how we are going to die, how to distribute our possessions, how to put our loved ones at ease emotionally, how to leave our legacy for future generations, how to share our stories to add meaning and purpose to our existence, or how to build resiliency and release regrets. In order to offer our most heartfelt gifts of healing and closure during the final days, it is important to learn how to have crucial, honest conversations with our loved ones. As we accept death with appreciation, we also invite passion.

More importantly, in attending to our death and its related issues, we give ourselves the freedom that allows us to live in the moment, live in joy, love wholeheartedly, and live with passion in everything we choose to do. When each day brings you the opportunity of living up to your potential, exploring your power, loving unabashedly, and serving your higher good, you are constantly creating the moments that matter with the people who matter while you still can. How does it get better than this?

Have you ever heard about someone who has almost died and then began living with kindness, vigor, passion, and purpose? There's a reason for this. Suddenly their life priorities became abundantly clear. Establishing clarity is the first thing a life coach does with a client too. Without clarity, we focus on many things, we partially achieve multiple goals, we allow obstacles to prevent us from reaching most of them, and it can easily seem as though we are just bouncing through life waiting for something important or different to come our way. Our real goal can be within reach and easily attainable, but without clarity we do not recognize it because we've never articulated it or defined it as a life priority.

So, whether it's relationships that have become rocky, combative, lethargic, and void of passion, physical symptoms that manifest in weight or health issues, careers that are stagnant, or finances that have prevented us from reaching our dreams, unresolved issues in life have a way of showing up in our time of death.

After retiring, I trained to be a hospice volunteer as my way of giving back. At some point I began to interview and capture the life stories of hospice patients and other elderly individuals. It was extremely rewarding and provided many opportunities to observe, learn, and better understand some of the things that become necessary when we know our days are numbered.

This is what I have learned. We each want to be heard. We want to know that our life had meaning and purpose. We want to release our regrets, forgive, and be forgiven. We want to express our love and know that we are loved. We want to share our stories and leave our legacy. We want to know that we matter.

As a life coach, the similarities and value of rewriting life situations and old stories are striking. Retelling our stories allows us the opportunity to notice inconsistencies, better understand our available choices along with our actions and behaviors, appreciate our accomplishments, value our history, and right our perceived shortcomings. This provides both healing and closure, not only for the person about to die, but also for the ones who will be left behind.

Emotions literally can make the difference between one's final days spent being terrified, angry, confused, frustrated, and vindictive or respectful, concerned, grieving, engaged, caring, supportive, and meaningful. This is a time when many families are driven apart—never to speak to each other again during their lifetimes—or it can be a time of healing and closure that brings new meaning to old stories and experiences.

In coaching families facing an impending death and end-of-life issues, I have designed two models to display how Emotional Levels and Engagement Levels (Model I: Quadrant) interact with the Circle of Choice (Model II). Briefly, you will notice that the quadrants were titled aptly to give you an indication of the impact of the individual and/or their family members based upon both the intersection of the type of emotions and the level of engagement/involvement with each other. End-of-life coaching provides opportunities to make some incredible changes to create the desired death experience.

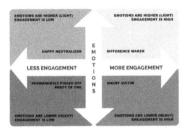

Model I: Emotions and Engagement   ***Model II: Hands of Choice***

Model I Angry Victim example: (person dying and/or family members) is very engaged, and displays Low/Heavy Emotions (anger, fear, bitterness, resentfulness, possessiveness, disappointment). **Actions** *may include volatile outbursts, legal actions, fighting, argumentative behavior, and disruptiveness.* **Outcomes:** *missed opportunities, negative emotional aftermaths, feuding/bickering long after death, no closure, and low emotions remain for all involved.*

Fortunately, even the Angry Victim family can be easily guided to become Difference Makers. To learn more, I am available for coaching, workshops, retreats, and speaking engagements; you can reach me at www.drjanetb.com/schedule.

Dr. Janet Bieschke, *life coach, author, and inspirational speaker, retired after decades in the corporate world and now assists those ready to make life changes with ease, joy, and grace while they create peace of heart and mind. She brings peace to those facing an impending death and also to their loved ones. She and her husband, Richard, live in rural Wisconsin.*

www.drjanetb.com

JOURNEY TO BECOMING PAIN-FREE

The Power of Listening

Laura Booker

Not many people know the level of suffering I experienced day in and day out. I woke up in pain, I pushed through the day in pain, and at night, although I tried to sleep, all I did was toss and turn for hours in pain!

I was at my lowest point. I was defeated. I had no hope for recovery and no imminent answers as to what to do to solve this problem. I had seen every doctor you could think of from back specialists to rheumatologists. Technicians x-rayed every part of my body. I underwent eight MRIs, tried a variety of medications, but nothing worked or even helped a little bit.

Excruciating chronic pain was my life for seventeen years (from the age of twenty to thirty-seven). It started out with small aches and pains here and there, then gradually moved to joint and spine pain, and finally to muscle and pressure point pain all over my body. My activity level was very limited. Due to the increased pain I would experience post-workout, my muscle recovery process would last for days. I lived with chronic back and body pain for many many years before I finally found hope and listened to my own inner wisdom to become PAIN-FREE.

From the time I was a young girl to becoming an active business-woman and mother, my physical and emotional body went through a lot of trauma. I suffered physical pain when I raced down a mountain and crashed at 50 kilometers per hour; I suffered emotional pain from a teenage rape; and I suffered mental/neurological pain caused by two major, life-threatening car accidents, one keeping me homebound with a TBI for eleven months. I worked through a bankruptcy, and I survived the loss of many lovers and friends. You name it, I went through it on my journey to discover the answer to living pain-free. By sharing my lessons, awakenings, wisdom, and experience with you, I hope to be able to save you future physical, emotional, and spiritual pain.

Nine years ago, at age thirty-one, I sat on the couch with a hot water bottle heating my aching lower back, again trying to recover from the stress of day and the low energy I felt from not sleeping the night before. My eighteen-month-old daughter Sophie crawled up on the couch beside me, looked up at me, put her hand on my forearm, and started rubbing it back and forth, back and forth, trying to console me. Oblivious to what she was doing, I pulled her close and said, "Oh honey, come cuddle Mommy."

The next night, it was the same routine: barely able to get off the couch, trying to minimize the chronic pain with the hot water bottle on my back. Sophie once again crawled up on the couch; this time she took her tiny little arm, put it behind my shoulder, placed her hand on my back and started rubbing it up and down, trying to console and comfort me. At this moment I finally realized what she was doing—my little girl who couldn't even talk yet was trying to make me feel better. She could see that I was in pain and wanted to help me.

Let's just say in that moment it was as though I had been hit by lightning. I told myself, *NO MORE! It's not my little girl's job to console me or take care of me—it's my job to look after her.*

And how was I going to do that if I couldn't even take care of myself?

Right then and there, I took my daughter in my arms and said, "I'm READY! I'm ready for teachers to come into my life; I'm ready to listen and learn whatever I need to figure out in order to heal my pain so I can be the best mother I can be to the most amazing little girl."

That was over nine years ago. After suffering seventeen years of excruciating chronic pain (what Western medicine tried to diagnose as fibromyalgia, arthritis, or whatever other label they could come up), I am pain-free. How did I do it?

That's where hope comes in. Once I listened, *really listened*, to my body, all the answers revealed themselves to me.

No matter what you might be going through, you already have all the answers. You just need to listen, and you will be set free too.

Where do you start? How do you listen?

1.   Be vulnerable, be hopeful, and ask for the teachers to come.
2.   Sit with yourself, quiet your mind, meditate, and be mindful.
3.   Forgive, let go, allow, and release.

4. Discover tools to help you listen (all kinds of options exist); find what works for you.
5. Tell yourself and believe you are worthy of being pain-free.
6. Receive the healing; accept the gifts.
7. Learn to let go of past negative energy, and learn how to allow future energy to flow through you.
8. Accept and love yourself; you are enough.
9. Embrace the journey of life.
10. Love yourself.

For those of you who have given up, who see no light at the end of the tunnel, please hear my words and find hope again. If anyone was lost and ready to give up, it was me. Seventeen years of pain and no answers has a way of bringing you down.

I was fortunate enough to be reminded of the opportunities life has for me—and to know that I am 100 percent responsible for that experience.

Please listen to yourself and accept the gifts and healers who will come into your life. You are worthy; you are beautiful; you are perfect!

If you only take one little tidbit away from this message, please always have hope. Don't give up! There is an answer for whatever you are experiencing, and you will find a way through it.

Laura Booker is an educated, award-winning, extroverted alpha female. She is mother-in-training to a beautiful soul, Sophie. She is an aspiring serial entrepreneur, a student of life who is interested in giving back and expanding consciousness. She plans to retire on a cruise line, teaching contract bridge and yoga.

THE ETERNAL WELL
OF CREATIVITY

Ruth Broyde Sharone

It was all quite mysterious. It began in the fall of 2014. During my daily walks I started to hear melodies in my head that seemed to erupt, complete with lyrics, like fully formed children. The first song that popped out was openly playful and made me laugh out loud.

What if, when you awoke, you were wearing a stranger's shoes?
What if, when you awoke, you shared your enemy's extremist views?
What if, when you awoke, you'd think in color—not black or white?
What if, when you awoke, you could imagine not being right!

The subject matter was not surprising. After thirty years of working in the field of interfaith engagement, I had come to recognize that diversity and empathy are our greatest strengths and ultimately our greatest gifts to the planet. By harnessing the brilliance and genius contained within our diversity and by acknowledging our shared humanity, I sincerely believe we can achieve world peace and find solutions to the greatest challenges of our times.

First, however, we need to be able to imagine what it's like to inhabit a stranger's shoes.

Throughout the years of my interfaith adventures, I had frequently contemplated the theme of tribal prejudices that keep us separate and alienated from one another. But I was still bewildered about the source of the song. It seemed more like a message from another realm rather than from my own interior landscape and experience.

Then I remembered something I had read when I was a teenager in *The Prophet* by Lebanese writer Khalil Gibran. Asked to speak about the relationship between parents and children, he responded: "Your children are not your children. . . . They come through you but not from you. . . . And though they are with you yet they belong not to you." I couldn't help wondering if the songs I was hearing in my head really belonged to me.

25

Although I played piano for many years, I had always felt most at home as an author and documentary filmmaker, expressing myself through the written word and the language of film. I never considered myself a song-writer, but that was about to change—and so was my life.

The chorus for the song tumbled out next, and in my mind's eye, I saw a standing-room-only audience representing all religions, ethnicities, races, and creeds.

What if. . .what if . . . what if we all could see . . .
The beauty of one expanding humanity?

In the two years that followed, I wrote some thirty songs during my walks (and they are still coming to me), including both serious and amusing lyrics. I shared my songs with my good friend Yuval Ron, a composer-musician and founder of an international interfaith ensemble. "You're writing a musical," he said. "Did you know that?"

No, I hadn't noticed. But I recognized my desire to reach out beyond the boundaries of my interfaith community right into the heart of mainstream America. I felt sure the general public would be drawn to a musical perfor-mance with a great story, and so I began to develop an interfaith story about love and longing, hope and doubt, conflict and fulfillment. Perhaps people who had no direct knowledge of interfaith matters could be enticed into an auditorium where—through the irresistible power of music and the theater arts—they could first acknowledge, and then celebrate, the scope and beauty of our diversity.

I had long ago discovered the arts to be the most powerful vehicle avail-able to convey our shared humanity, and I always made a point of includ-ing music and film when I presented on college campuses and in multiple community settings. I would specifically invite singers and musicians and dancers of diverse ethnic and religious backgrounds to perform together as a way to demonstrate harmony-in-action.

Yuval recommended a very talented young arranger, KC Daugirdas, and within a year, on a limited budget, I released an album with eleven of the thirty songs I had written. *INTERFAITH: The Musical* was becom-ing a reality. Soon I began performing the songs publicly to enthusiastic audiences who resonated deeply with the subject matter. They laughed and they cried—and I hadn't even completed the libretto for the musical. "Broadway-bound on the wings of peace," was my tagline.

But then I had a major psychological setback. While participating in "Boot

Camp for New Musicals," I was advised to put aside all of my songs and just write the story. "There are songs you have written that won't fit the story," my teacher explained, "and then there will be new songs you'll have to compose."

I remember going into a panic. Write new songs? How would I do that when the songs I had already written had not been consciously planned? They just seemed to come through me, out of nowhere. I suddenly felt paralyzed in my work. I stopped writing my story outline, feeling incapable of continuing. I didn't even know the basics of musical theater. How could I presume to write a musical? "You're a filmmaker and writer, not a songwriter and playwright," said an accusing voice in my head. I faced a crisis of confidence entirely new to me.

It took me weeks to recover from my teacher's comment. When I did, however, it was with a new concept about creativity that I believe applies to everyone in every stage of life—from childhood through the golden years.

Creativity is an eternal well from which we all can draw, a well of pure potential that exists beyond time and space and is always available to us. This inexhaustible well has everything we might ever need—even when we aren't yet aware of our needs.

That night I sat down and intentionally wrote a song.

I feel confident that whatever song I will need to write, I can write. Whatever I need to learn, I will learn. I understand now that creativity has no limits.

Honored internationally for her interfaith activism and leadership, filmmaker and journalist **Ruth Broyde Sharone** *is the creator of* INTERFAITH: The Musical. *A contributor to the* Huffington Post *and the* Interfaith Observer, *Ruth co-chaired the Southern California Parliament of the World's Religions for ten years. She also pioneered groundbreaking interfaith pilgrimages to the Middle East. Her documentary* God and Allah Need to Talk *and her interfaith memoir,* Minefields & Miracles, *have received multiple awards.*

www.interfaiththemusical.com

JOURNEY TO
A BRIGHT FUTURE

Your Genes Don't Have to Be Your Destiny

Christi Christiaens

I am Christi, and I used to have a severe drug addiction. No, not cocaine or heroin, but another potent, crystalline substance obtained from various plants—sugar. Studies have shown that sugar is as addictive as cocaine, and our society promotes its consumption!

After years of struggling, I uncovered the root cause of my addiction and finally was released from my sugar prison. I became free to live my life as a healthy, energized, and powerful woman. My obsessive craving for sugar ended, and I experienced a peace of mind that I didn't realize existed.

I was born and raised in Belgium in the post-World-War II era. My grandfather was a renowned pastry chef with his own shop. Succulent, handcrafted desserts were a way of life, mainly as a reaction to the famine my relatives had to endure in surviving the war. My entire family was addicted to sugar. And it wasn't just sweets, either. I was raised on an excessive diet of bread, which only feeds the cycle because it turns to sugar once consumed.

Both my grandmothers, as well as my mother, were overweight and had Type 2 diabetes, a dreadful modern disease that is becoming epidemic. My paternal grandmother had her leg amputated due to complications of her disease. I was a young girl at the time and was deeply shocked at the loss of her leg. I also witnessed her diminished quality of life due to depression. She died when I was twelve, and I was devastated by her death. It was a turning point in my life.

I vividly remember thinking, *This can't be what life is about!* I decided then and there that I was going to do everything I could to prevent weight gain and what felt like a diabetic destiny.

I wanted to be an artist. I spent all my free time drawing and painting and eventually became a graphic designer. I loved that creative outlet, but I was truly fascinated by and drawn to the world of nutrition. I studied everything I could get my hands on and experimented with just about every diet out there.

In my late twenties, with several nutritional certificates in hand, I began a journey involving food and health. I taught cooking classes in a health food store, and I owned a health food restaurant.

In the years that followed, I lived in several European countries. In the South of France, I worked as a chef in a beautiful mountain resort/ranch. It was a great pleasure to prepare foods for the guests. I just had to walk to the garden to harvest fresh, organic veggies and fruits. In Spain my then-husband and I owned a plantation that produced almonds, olives, grapes, and oranges.

Back in Belgium, when I was in my forties, I had a deep desire to help women become and stay healthy and fit. I opened a wellness studio for women and taught nutrition and exercise, but I felt like a fraud because I still had uncontrollable sugar and carb cravings. I relied on extreme willpower and exercise to control my weight and my sugar cravings. At the same time, I went through a divorce that took longer than expected. I knew deep inside that I couldn't keep up the willpower much longer, and I went through an emotional roller coaster. And all this time I was raising four children, battling their sugar cravings as well as mine.

With 100 percent dedication, I started researching and studying the science and psychology of food cravings and sugar addiction. I discovered the answers and finally, after several attempts, I conquered my cravings for good! Like any drug addict, I did go through a short period of withdrawal and cravings. But to my surprise, I didn't feel deprived; instead I felt nourished and had more sustainable energy and focus.

During this stage of my journey, I surrounded myself with many like-minded people, and along the way I met some inspiring folks who were part of a super-longevity community, People Unlimited. I was so drawn to them that I made the decision to join their community in Phoenix, Arizona, leaving my life in Belgium behind.

At age fifty, I landed in Phoenix with two suitcases, ready to start a new life. During the first year, I experienced a true "culture shock." Fortunately I was surrounded by supportive, caring people. These people challenge the status quo regarding health, aging, and lifespan. We meet twice a week in Scottsdale, Arizona, and every year we celebrate our commitment to extending health and well-being at RAADfest (Revolution Against Aging and Death), where we learn about the latest scientific advancements on health and age reversal. Many new innovations and modalities are discussed, including stem cells, molecular biology, telomeres, gene therapy, and epigenetics.

Most of us have been led to believe that our genes doom us to the diseases that run in our family. While we can't change the genes we were born with, we can change how they affect us. Our genes respond to our diet, lifestyle, and environment.

My gene-testing results indicated that I have multiple genes related to a high risk of diabetes and obesity. However, I proved that genetic doom theory wrong! I am not overweight, and my blood sugar levels are in the perfect range. I couldn't change my genetics, but I did change my diet, lifestyle, and environment.

I have continued my quest in the US, helping women to conquer cravings, lose weight, and feel better than ever regardless of age. I don't believe in quick-fix diets—they simply don't work. It takes a transformation from the inside out! Diet alone isn't enough; the emotional aspect needs to be addressed as well.

As a child I saw the devastating effects of disease on people I dearly loved. Deep inside I believed that we were able to take charge of our health through diet, lifestyle, and environment. And so we are!

Christi Christiaens is a certified health/nutrition coach, motivational speaker, and author. Originally from Belgium and having lived in several European countries, Christi's international experience contributes greatly to her unique style of coaching. She combines over thirty-five years of experience with dedicated study in the areas of brain chemistry, neuropsychology, epigenetics, and anti-aging. Her expertise in these fields enables her to facilitate a true transformation in her clients' well-being.

www.coachwithchristi.com

RELENTLESS

Lache pas la patate

Elizabeth M. Clamon

Be relentless! Never give up! No matter what hardships you may face, dig deep within yourself and find the strength and courage to continue.

Often relentlessness can be thought of as a negative; however, I think of relentlessness as a positive. It's the quality of being tenacious, of holding fast, of being persistent. That's how I am—tenacious, relentless.

I have always been relentless for as long as I can remember. Some might call it stubbornness, but my journey on this planet hasn't been an easy one, therefore requiring me to be tenacious. Being born to a single mother in 1965, raised until I was six as my grandparents' child, losing my grandfather suddenly at age five, and then just six months later being taken from my grandmother and the only home and family I had ever known would have broken someone who wasn't tenacious.

It didn't break me, nor did the other blows this life had in store for me. Living in the home of my biological mother and stepfather after being taken from my grandmother, I was emotionally, mentally, and at times physically abused. I was also sexually abused by my stepbrothers when I was nine years old. I have always had a God-given ability to endure whatever hardships came my way and continue to persevere.

At age eighteen I defied my entire family to marry my husband, a man I had only been dating for four months. I knew in my heart, without a doubt, that it was the best thing for me. We have been happily married for thirty-three years now. My relentlessness and tenacity paid off again.

I have drawn on those attributes, as well as my faith, throughout my life. It has not been an easy path, but it's been one I have traveled with grit and determination. From the loss of our first and third pregnancies, which was completely heartbreaking, to living with chronic illness and pain, I some-how have found the strength to carry on.

In my thirties all the childhood abuse I had suffered came rushing at me like a tide of deep, dark water that threatened to take me under. It was a tumultuous time of complete brokenness that I had to grieve through and recover from. I spent months alternating between depression and anger. Years of counseling were required to overcome the onslaught of emotional pain that had scarred me.

Unfortunately, my family of origin did not believe me, and we ended up going our separate ways. This was by far the hardest thing I have had to go through, but I had to be relentless in order to heal my mind, body, emo-tions, and spirit. Sometimes self-healing requires making difficult decisions and putting yourself first.

Healing was hard work, and I was making good progress when I faced my biggest challenge. It came in the form of an auto accident. My hus-band, children, and I were traveling back from a family camping trip, when suddenly in the midst of rush-hour traffic, we were confronted with a semitruck that had abruptly stopped on the highway in front of us. Unable to stop while towing a loaded camper, we hit the semi, our camper hit us from behind, and our sixteen- and eighteen-year-old daughters, following in our truck, hit the camper.

Trapped in our vehicle, underneath the semi, injured, and in shock, I couldn't even get myself out of my seat belt. My husband kicked out a window and extracted us from the vehicle. My family walked away with bruises, minor cuts, and burns, but I spent five days in the cardiac ward.

Multiple injuries, years of physical therapy, seven surgeries, disabil-ity, and twelve years of being bedridden is what I had to overcome this time. My final surgery was the last straw. Unable to control my pain and going into shock, I dug down deep inside and drew on the Cajun spirit of *lache pas la patate* and decided I was done! After recovering from that surgery, I used my training in naturopathic healing and made a plan for my healing.

With relentlessness and tenacity, I gained a level of healing that now enables me to pursue my dreams of being an entrepreneur, professional speaker, and coach. I owe it all to God who made me to be relentless, tena-cious, and overcoming.

Elizabeth M. Clamon, *a naturopath, is living proof that natural healing works. She has not only survived, but thrived, despite childhood abuse, chronic illness, and being left disabled and bedridden for twelve years from an auto accident. She provides an insightful, inspirational, and educational experience to inspire people to overcome obstacles and live their dreams.*

www.elizabethclamon.com

"Because" Is Not an Answer

Deb Coman

My dad always insisted, "'Because' is not an answer" when my sisters and I would respond to his questions halfheartedly with "Because." As a teen it was so annoying (insert eye roll) to have to expand on it. Why couldn't the short answer be enough? But this was Dad, and he "didn't take 'no' for an answer," so I'd have to come up with some long-form reply. Then I'd stomp up the few blue carpeted steps of our Long Island split-level in my Earth shoes and bell-bottoms. Of course, more than once I had to "come right back down here and walk up the stairs without stomping."

He was a smidgen strict, and I was the mostly-do-as-I'm-told-but-occasionally-defiant oldest. After all, I had two younger sisters; someone had to pave the way! I'm sure I never said it back then, but Dad was right on so many levels. As an adult it's much easier for me to admit that, while I don't always have to tell everyone the why behind my answer, I do need to understand it fully myself. It's how I make choices with intention and not let life just happen any which way it feels like happening.

Little did I know then how much my dad's pursuit of my why would impact my life. As a woman business owner, knowing my why and digging deeper than "because" is the way I've attracted clients and developed all my business relationships. Once I fully knew my why, it shaped all my messaging and inspired me to succeed. It now has become an integral part of what I empower my clients to do.

My core message? I'm a content conversion strategist, copywriter, and speaker who empowers business owners to get clear about their message and use strategy to share it in a way that attracts ideal clients and converts them to sales and referrals. And the "why" behind my core message? It's simple: my family; my husband; my boys; my desire for a flexible business that gives me time to spend with them; and the ability to work on projects I choose, with people I choose, when I want to, and from wherever in the the world I want to work.

At first I didn't know how I "should" show up online. My default was all I had . . . to just be myself. I emailed people whose websites I found online and asked if they needed help with writing or editing. I shared my core message and had conversations. Complete strangers from all over the world became clients. My core message and the why that drove it was enough.

Now I teach this same process, and it's one of my favorite things to do.

I absolutely love helping business owners discover their why and how their core message—the one that exists as a feeling, wordless and unspoken in their minds and in their hearts—is their most compelling marketing material. My close second favorite thing? Helping them to catch the end of that thread and pull gently to gradually, patiently coax it out, taking care not to alter it from its pure, natural state. I call it getting grounded in your core purpose and message.

It brings me joy to support people this way and to witness the noticeable relief in their faces when they realize they can trust that the words that come to them with ease are enough.

We forgo the common practice of dressing up simple language until it sounds like something we'd never say. We don't cram it into marketing templates where it loses its purity and authenticity (as would we if we were put through that same process). That way is stressful, exhausting, and ineffective in the long run. We're all tired of trying to sound a certain way. We've had it with staying on top of the latest favorite marketing terms so we can struggle to weave them into our message. We want the freedom to be who we really, truly are. And I don't even like to call this *authenticity* because the word itself has become tainted and worn out from overuse. As if when we say we're authentic, we must be. And those who claim it most emphatically seem to be moving further and further away from it.

When we are truly authentic, we don't have to say it so often. When we show up and speak and write and market in the language that comes from our hearts, we are as real as it gets—and that doesn't need a buzzword to describe it. It just "is."

Showing up real and in our own words is an effective marketing strategy that helps us stand out. A successful client pathway is paved with our content . . . our words. Along the path there must be an exchange. Value must be given, trust must be transferred, and an interaction must occur. There is no shortcut. There is no faking it. There are people—real people—at the other end of our message.

When I first started my business, I wrote marketing copy on the clunky, slow desktop computer in the basement at night after my boys went to sleep two floors up. I can still remember the almost giddy excitement as I hurried down the brown carpeted steps in slip-on shoes and yoga pants to the stack of manila folders filled with notes I would use to help people dig beneath their why to grow their business.

And these days when I help clients with their why, I still feel the thrill. The why behind my why is that I care about their message. I care that they are being seen by the people they're meant to serve. I care that they are being heard. I care that their message tells their clients what it's like to work with them, what it is they care about, why they do what they do, and what their intent is.

I help them finish their "because . . ."

Deb Coman *is a content conversion strategist, copywriter, and speaker. She empowers business owners to create, share, and repurpose compelling messaging and content that attracts and converts. Delivering a comprehensive online presence that aligns with core values and builds relationships, Deb supports clients to simplify their marketing. As part of the Leadership Team at Women Speakers Association, Deb thrives in its spirit of connection and collaboration.*

www.debcoman.com

INSPIRING POSSIBILITIES

Conquer Fear, Let Go of Perfection, and Jump into Your Greatness

Michelle Cameron Coulter

*"The earth is two-thirds water; you're going to come into contact with it
one of these days . . . so you better learn how to swim!"*
—*Jackie Cameron, my mom*

Growing up in a blended family of ten kids, I learned about teamwork, being flexible, and always finding a way. Given my mom's view about water, learning how to swim was not an option! The biggest challenge for me, though, was that I hated the water! I was so afraid that I failed my first level *four* times!

On my fourth attempt, I jumped and turned around to grab the side of the pool out of fear, and *boom!* cracked my chin on the edge and quickly descended to the bottom of the deep end.

As I sat on the bottom, a strange sensation came over me: I totally relaxed. It was peaceful; it really was not so bad, and I slowly floated up to the surface. When we totally relax, we will float. When we are stressed and *fearful,* we sink. What a huge life lesson for me to learn at that time! Never in a million years would anyone have thought that this quiet, shy, sickly little kid who was so afraid would go on to own the podium and win an Olympic Gold Medal for her country in the sport of Synchronized *Swimming!*

I started my sport late, at thirteen years old. A few years later, I made the senior swim team—not because I was good enough, but because they needed another swimmer. I never swam to try and beat anyone; I just focused on doing a little better every day, and the results started to come.

1984 was the first year our sport was in the Olympics. The following year I was paired with the Olympic silver medalist, and we went to our first World Championships together. We trained six to eight hours a day. We had a tough yet extremely amazing coach. We were one of the first teams to work with exercise physiologists and psychologists. They utilized peak performance testing and helped us maximize the massive exertion and precision required while holding our breath for 70 percent of a four-minute routine.

A pivotal moment for me came weeks before Worlds when my coach stopped me in the middle of a drill underwater and said, "How would you do it if you were already a World Champion?" Wow! This switch in mindset changed everything for me.

Our main competition was a pair of identical twins who had been swimming together for sixteen years. Not only that, the championships took place in their hometown, in a pool with ten thousand spectators. Against all the odds, we went on to win our first World Championship. Confidence comes from doing! We would go on to be undefeated three years in a row, until the twins beat us at a pre-Olympic meet, months before the Olympic games in Seoul, Korea. We went back to the drawing board, analyzed our strengths, and focused on what made us better. We worked harder than ever, and finally we were ready for the pinnacle, the Olympic games. With the world watching, I caught one set of eyes in the stands of thousands right before we swam—it was my mom. Everything came together at that moment: we would own the podium; the Olympic Gold Medal was ours!

Realizing such a huge dream came with a dark cost, however. As women, we are all so hard on ourselves—and participating in a judged sport wearing a bathing suit only amplifies this. We would eat next to nothing—not nearly enough for the amount we trained. I remember one day a coach saying to me, "Oh look, you're getting fat." Already self-conscious about needing to be perfect, I had heard rumors about throwing up to try and stay thin, and I decided that must be the only way. "I've got this," I told myself. It was simple . . . until it wasn't. I didn't have it—it had me.

The more nervous I was, the harder it became and the greater the feeling of shame if anyone found out. The last five years of my swimming career, I battled with bulimia. After the Olympics my issues with food continued and only got worse. I gained almost thirty pounds the first year I finished swimming. My metabolism was so screwed up. I was traveling all over and doing amazing things and yet still beating myself up.

My first wake-up call came when I had been married for two years and we were expecting our first baby—I had a miscarriage. I was devastated. It was time for me to take care of myself. I was blessed to be pregnant again literally three months later, and I went on to have four amazing children, three girls and a boy. I struggled with my self-image and my eating disorder off and on throughout that time. Often I would openly complain and cut myself down.

My second wake-up call came when I saw the impact this was having on my girls! I made the decision to take care of myself. I finally was on the road to recovery. A few years later, the biggest weight lifted physically and emotionally when my oldest daughter was in university studying psychology. She was doing a research project on girls in sport—particularly judged sport—and the high rate of eating disorders. She called me and asked me if I thought that was true. We had the best heart-to-heart! I never wanted my girls to go through what I went through. I didn't want them to be so hard on themselves and worry about what other people think.

One of my fears was that, in my sharing "my secret," I would feel unworthy of the accomplishments I had attained in my life in sport and beyond. Just the opposite happened, though. It has allowed me to be much more connected, stronger, empowered, and real, and I am able to authentically inspire others to be their best, explore their incredible possibilities, and create their own *gold medal results*. What are we capable of when we let go of our fears, let go of perfection, and uninhibitedly jump into our greatness? And bonus—actually have FUN!

I now have the privilege and honor of speaking all over the world on Inspiring Possibilities and the Gold Medal Potential we all have and can achieve in a healthy and vibrant way. Life's challenges make us who we are, and for that I am ultimately grateful. *Being a champion is not about being the best in the world—it's about being the best we can be and being real in the process.*

Michelle Cameron Coulter, *CEO and founder of Inspiring Possibilities, is the embodiment of today's woman. Strong and empowering, she has embraced life's challenges with strength and courage. She brings insight, compassion, depth, and inspiration to the table, with six World Championships, an Olympic gold medal, marriage, four children, a successful inspirational speaking, workshop, and retreat business among her many accomplishments.*

www.michellecameroncoulter.com

YOUR MIND IS A GOLD MINE

Veronica A. Cunningham

When asked if there were one lesson learned or story I'd like to leave as a legacy, I had to pause and ponder because there have been countless lessons learned and incredible stories over the years. Then I thought of the binding thread of commonality interwoven throughout every lesson, every story. And I realized there really is only one story with different dynamics and one common denominator: *the mind.*

Our minds desire freedom and need to be free to imagine and create. If our minds are bound by stress, frustration, agony, or self-sabotaging thoughts, we become stifled by their constriction. A wealth of possibilities resides inside our minds, but we can only access it through an unobstructed path. Many of us obstruct our own paths with fear, anxiety, doubts, and worries that prevent entry to the core of our most prized possession.

What connects us is our resonating experiences, our compassion, and our humanity. The triumph of the human spirit is astounding when challenged beyond what it thinks itself incapable of surpassing. Everything depends on how our minds perceive something. Those perceptions impact feelings, which too often race to the driver's seat.

Everything is breakable, destructible, or damageable. Even the strongest of us can crack under the right pressure! Our minds have a breaking point when overloaded, which is why mining our minds is crucial. What we tell ourselves and what we actually believe are not always harmonious; therefore, affirmations should be based on core beliefs instead of trendy jargon. The inner work of clarifying, supporting, even redefining our core beliefs should be continual because habits become patterns—and patterns create lifestyles. Do you want a Champion lifestyle?

Champions train their minds for resiliency to bounce back *quickly* from perceived failure, rejection, and knockdowns. We all can discipline our minds to focus on solutions rather than situations.

Developing a Champion Mindset—Top Five High-Level Checklist:
1. Disengage Distractions (in whatever form they appear)
2. Nullify Negative Thoughts (replace with uplifting ones immediately)
3. Vocalize a Victorious Vocabulary (positive affirmations you genuinely believe)
4. Remain Optimistically Grateful (despite circumstances and conditions)
5. Conceive–BELIEVE–Achieve (feed what fuels your belief)

So what feedback would I give my younger self? Love more, live more, give more, and forgive more. I didn't always love freely, live courageously, give generously, or forgive readily. Humbling life travails that took me to the edge and had me searching for deeper meaning led me to a revelatory self-examination process. Through my odysseys, I became more compassionate and committed to personal development and a higher level of authenticity.

Peace of mind is an inside job. Acknowledging we are all perfectly human and humanly flawed, I chose to paint the picture of who I authentically am, working from the inside out to actualize the life of that image. Over time, with God and continual activity in mind mining, consciousness elevation, and self-discovery, I progressed to honoring the Champion in me. A paradigm shift was merely the genesis to produce change; I have to walk it out every day, in every way through the wildernesses. It became imperative for me to immerse myself in what I desired, envisioned, and believed without being derailed by distractions. This immersion required ACTION steps, not wandering wishes. And I needed the freedom to be *all* of me.

Lastly, discover and engage your cathartic channel and stop at nothing until you succeed. My creative catalyst for inner cleansing and healing is soul-depth self-expression—putting pen to paper crafting poetry, prose, and social commentary, which I have been honored to recite on international stages and present to dignitaries. *Freedom* is a journey from a mind of agony to a mind of victory!

Freedom

From the shadows of the tombs that swallowed fizzling hope
Peeps desperation—isolation—trepidation—determination
Of what fallacy was the fantasy that acquiesced into obscurity?
One that held captive sunbeams—sunrises—and my imagination
The rise/the fall/the climb/the slip/the momentum/stagnation
In whose court may I plead my case for freedom?

No jingle bell rock on the red-eye roller coaster inside my mind
Where the real odyssey breeds and my seared soul bleeds
A hemorrhaging heart yet refusing to cease the beats
Steps to stride whose identity is a daring familiar stranger
Distraught—a life of purpose sought while excruciation wrought

In whose court may I plead my case for freedom?

Those staring eyes of disappointment that haunt me
The subconscious tales and realities that nightly taunt me
The vacillating circular thoughts that almost consumed me
While vision vampires parade and promenade to distract me
But the reverb of the words I speak empower me
In whose court may I plead my case for freedom?

I need to believe the rainbow beyond ALL I feel and see
Beyond the blades that sliced me and cut me deep
Beyond the poisonous vapors that appeared to seize me
Beyond every rejection, heartbreak, and casualty
Beyond staggering loss, uncertainty, and tragedy
In whose court may I plead my case for freedom?

Truth scattered the ashes and burst through the dragnet
Burning moons of tribulation, terror, trauma, and grief
Uncovering—rediscovering essence/passion/audacity
An evolution of a revolution deferred by distress
Destiny dared call again and again and I arose to answer
In whose court may I plead my case for freedom?

I *choose* to believe the rainbow beyond ALL I feel and see
The price was paid repeatedly as we awaited the cavalry
Attempts at hope held hostage are met with antiquity
Remembering how my ancestors overcame atrocities
Love awakened, lighting a path to peace and equanimity
And I became witness, jury, and judge, and set myself free.

Freedom.

Veronica A. Cunningham *is a multi-award-winning video and cablecast producer, spoken word recording/performance artist, inspirational speaker, songwriter, poet, transformational life coach, and author of* Crushed But Not Conquered: A Guide to Celebrating the Champion in You. *An insightful soul, Veronica helps others discover their gifts, create change, and develop a Champion Mindset. She conducts women's empowerment sessions, and believes life is a laboratory of learning.*

www.veronicacunningham.com

MY INVINCIBLE TRUTH

Andrea Dawn

We are all weird in some way, but when we hide who we are, we suffer. My story is not better or worse than any others; it just is. I am not a role model and am by no means perfect, but I'm ready and willing to fully share my truth. My life experiences include dysfunction, divorce, molestation with child pornography victimization, drugs, rape, abortion, religious zealousness, homeschooling, and spiritual alchemy. It might be easy to see some aspects of my life experience as traumatic and difficult, but I invite you to look at it as a healing journey that has left me feeling totally free.

As a child I used anger to overcome my fear. As a teenager I used drugs and alcohol to suppress my feelings. As an adult I used work to avoid my insecurities, and I used being a wife and mother as an excuse to not face the truth of who I was and what I wanted.

I've learned that there is nothing we can't overcome. From the outside looking in, people have always thought I was a bit different. I quickly learned to be a chameleon and mask the very things that made me unique. When I look back now, I can see that everything happened for a reason, and that reason was meant to support me. While it was happening, though, I really believed I was crazy. My psychic abilities and my chaotic family looked different from those of my peers. My authentic self was hidden. Mediumship, spirituality, and intuition were the things I tried so hard to hide, and now they make up my livelihood.

In 2014 I separated for the first time from my soon-to-be ex-husband. One might see my separation as just another statistic, but spiritually it was an integral part of my awakening. Having spent the majority of my marriage adhering to the guidelines of religious doctrine, my misguided beliefs kept me imprisoned until I realized that I was deserving of love.

I told myself I would stay in the relationship long enough for my girls to reach adulthood. I didn't expect a memory of sexual abuse to throw me into a spiral of awareness, but when that memory showed itself to me, I began to unravel. Feeling distressed and confused, I spoke to my husband about what I was remembering. His immediate verbal response to me was, "So does that mean we're not having sex for awhile?" I was so dumbfounded that it left me, the talker, without words. We all say things without thinking at times. However, his comment during such a vulnerable moment really stood out and demonstrated exactly how our relationship had been for the past twenty-two years. I'd love to say that I had an aha moment and ended the marriage immediately. The reality was that I went back to him after that first separation. Eventually we separated again and ultimately divorced.

How did I get out of my broken marriage? I still don't have an exact answer to that. I know it took a desire to want more for myself and my children, personal development conversations and classes, and an absolute commitment to truly know myself. This commitment to really know myself was the most impactful decision. I remember crying in the car after my final therapy session and saying aloud, "No matter what, I just want to know who I am."

Somehow, this proclamation, stated with conviction from deep within, put in motion the chain of events that would follow. Every new step brought me more and more awareness. I was guided to understand that there really is only one thing I must do to live an awakened life, and that is to love. Love myself, love every choice I make, love every experience I have. Just love.

There is an innate truth within us that serves as our ultimate knowing. We know what we know, and we can't un-know it. Throughout all the years of that marriage, we lived in the dysfunctional behaviors carried forward from childhood. Still, I had a knowing that I could not be in the marriage for the rest of my life. Did that make it wrong or bad? No, it was our journey to be married for as long as we were.

My knowing is that we live free when we love more expansively. In my role as a spiritual alchemist, I often give one-on-one or group readings. At the start of the reading, I always say, "I am only here to confirm what you already know." My clients, just like you, are always being guided to find their truth, their voice, their bliss, and ultimately live a life of love.

Learning to replace fear with love felt so foreign to me at first. But little bit by little bit, it became fun and free. As I found my authentic self, I started down an entirely different path for my life. So many doors have now opened, such as becoming an author. These are doors I couldn't have even dreamed about with my old perspective. My soul is constantly evolving.

The more I stand in my truth, the more I find myself opening to new beliefs and experiences. My personal history, one that once held shame and judgment, is now one of love and healing.

When the Bible says that love covers a multitude of sins, it is really true. The root of sin is fear. When we love ourselves, we allow everyone else to be on their own journey, and we love them for it. We don't know what the homeless person's journey or life lesson is, for example, and we aren't meant to judge them or think that we are responsible to change things for them. We just need to love them for who they are right now.

I choose to have an expansive awareness of the multidimensional realm around me and share that awareness for the good and healing of others. At every group and one-on-one session, I learn something new, something Spirit reveals, shares, or allows me to explore in further detail. Most of all, I have had more miracles, magic, and fun since learning who I am.

I am not just a survivor or an overcomer—I am a thriver. I am genuinely free in every part of my life. There is no shame, no embarrassment; there is only love.

Andrea Dawn is a spiritual alchemist with a focus on healing and helping people to reach their highest, truest soul self. She channels and delivers guided messages. These messages can be: archangels, angels, animal guides, galactic friends, spirit guides, energy of the living, inter-dimensional lives, roads before you, and more.

www.awakeningswithandreadawn.com

BEAUTY AND FRAGILITY

Anne-Marie Dekker

I lost my "voice" in the second half of the first decade of this century. I lost my friend, my confidant, my constant guiding star, the love of my life . . . my husband.

Susan David says, "Life's beauty is inseparable from its fragility." So very true! There was beauty, serenity, and sacredness in our last good-bye, and there would be much fragility in the hours, then days, months, and years ahead. My life was turned upside down.

What does an upside-down life look like? It's new territory. New landscape. Suddenly there is nothing. Nothing. It's coming home, turning the doorknob, and having no one there to greet you, no one to ask how your day was. There is just silence. There is only emptiness.

Losing my husband was beyond anything I could have ever imagined, and imagining a life without him is something I often did during his last months. I was preparing myself for that eventual day—or so I thought. Preparing myself while he was still physically present is very different from when that final good-bye, those final words, were said and then no sound came back . . . ever again.

My husband often worried that he would die without having said thank you to me. Of course he did during our last hour together. What I didn't know then was how I'd later stumble on his truly final act to show me the love he constantly declared during our life together.

When I was finally able to go through his desk drawers, I found a simple black notebook with the word "Memo" in the center of the cover. I wondered what it could contain. As I opened the book and stared at the words and at his handwriting, I could feel myself holding my breath. Unbeknownst to me, he had written down all the nicknames he had given me during our life together. They were listed alphabetically, some with the story how a particular nickname originated. I cried uncontrollably upon the discovery. I held the book as if I were holding him. In that moment of nothingness, I experienced the meaning of Susan David's quote, the insep-arability of beauty and fragility.

I think back often to that moment of discovery. I can still see myself in that room. His office was his sanctuary. I stood by his desk. As I watched across the room the morning light filtering through the glass ceiling, sixteen feet high, my reluctance to disturb his personal items heightened.

I had postponed going through his desk for as long as I could. Rearranging the items on his desk seemed like some final act. My irrational mind told me if I moved any of the contents, I was dismantling his memory. *Our* memory.

While his loss wasn't unexpected, it had left me without a compass to find my next landscape. I was no longer a wife, no longer a partner in life and in business. What journey was I now on?

My interesting and diverse lineage and chance brought me to many parts of the world. I had enjoyed a global upbringing that stretched from Asia to Europe and then to the United States. In my early twenties I discov-ered Vancouver. I knew that city would become my home, and I immigrat-ed to Canada on my own.

Without family, I leaned on others to be my scaffold while I built a life in my new home city and country. The journey wasn't easy, nor was the road map always clear. I drew much on my instincts and the wisdom of my elders.

It may be necessary to stand on the outside if one is to see things clearly.
—Peter Høeg, *Tales of the Night*

Life in Vancouver produced a son and introduced me to the person I was destined to travel a life adventure with for thirty-one years. It should have been much longer. With his death, I found myself again standing on the outside.

There is beauty in brokenness. The Japanese have a practice called *kintsugi*, which means "golden joinery." It's the art of fixing broken ceramics with lacquer resin made to look like solid gold. Often the ceramic piece fixed by kintsugi will look more beautiful than the original. Would the discovery of the notebook become my practice of *kintsugi*? My new scaffold? My new compass? My new map? My new landscape?

W. Somerset Maughan says, "I do not bring back from a journey quite the same self that I took." What can I unlock from the experiences of life with my husband? What could I bridge between the self I was before to the self I am now on this new journey?

And the day came when the risk to remain tight in a bud
was more painful than the risk it took to blossom.
—Anaïs Nin

I am still adjusting, searching, and accepting what that self is or is yet to be. I bring part of my same self on this new journey. I will never let go of curiosity, of discovering endless possibilities. I will always aim for *shoshin*—a beginner's mind, a ready mind, open to everything. I will allow my map to change boundaries when necessary. I will continue to lean on many voices.

Beauty . . . fragility. While this new landscape often feels raw, incomplete, and frightening, there is power and beauty in this fragility. As Brother David Steindl-Rast says, "Be so still inside (yet vibrant) that you can listen at every moment to what life is offering you."

One of the few last words my husband said to me was to continue to stay involved in life and community. Today, I am honoring what was while exploring my new landscape—the landscape of helping others find their new frontiers.

Anne-Marie Dekker is a storycatcher and narrative coach. Her strength is being a connector, and she is insatiably curious about people and the world. She assists her clients to explore endless possibilities and build new frontiers. Previously she has helped create and run companies in the entertainment, broadcasting, and magazine publishing industries.

www.fourlovescoaching.com

You Have the Power to Rise Above

Tracey Ehman

When I graduated from high school, I never thought I would be where I am at today. I had visions of being a fashion designer and making the world more beautiful, and I guess in some ways I was able to accomplish that—albeit by taking a different path.

I was happily married, working full-time, and raising my children, but I was exhausted. I decided that it was time to make some changes. After working as a systems analyst at the same company for fifteen years, I felt I needed to spend more time with my children, so I went on a work hiatus. It wasn't long before I started missing that income, though, and I began seeking opportunities in direct sales that could provide some added cash. While I was only moderately successful with direct sales, what I did take away from that experience was the power of networking and community. Both direct sales and networking helped me get out of my comfort zone. I believe that if you look at things the right way, everything in life provides a learning experience.

Eventually I came to a fork in the road where I needed to decide if I was going to go back to my "day job" or use my inherent skills to work from home. This was a difficult time, and it was top of mind for many months. A decision needed to be made, but I struggled with the thought of going back to work full-time and missing that time with my children. This is where the community I built through networking came in. At a meeting I shared my thoughts and sought advice. By brainstorming, we talked about what I could offer, what my skills were, and where my joy came from when I was working in corporate. I loved taking tasks that appeared complicated and making them easier for people to understand. I had always found ways to basically translate "tech speak" into layman's terms, and I got joy from seeing a smile on my clients' faces when I understood what they had been struggling with. And what do you know? I walked away from that meeting with three clients and the decision to start my business as a virtual assistant.

Two years into my new business, I was on a roll, and then once again life stepped in and provided me with a challenge: I was diagnosed with breast cancer. My world seemed to stop. I felt so angry, so scared—my thoughts instantly went to all the things I might not see, such as my children's graduation, what they would achieve, who they would meet, whether they would get married, have children. . . . So many thoughts went through my mind. And suddenly so many things seemed unimportant.

As I navigated surgery and treatment, there were times when I thought I might need to put my business on hold, but I also knew I needed something to concentrate on so I wasn't dwelling on the "what ifs" all the time. Referrals continued to come in—in fact, they seemed to double. I have always been someone that is very truthful and authentic, so when I met with some of these potential new clients, I informed them of my diagnosis and upcoming treatment. I told them there were a lot of unknowns on my side, but my intention was to work between chemo treatments. After a treatment I would likely be down for seventy-two hours, so communication would be the key to making our partnership a success. I also gave them an out, telling them that they were welcome to find someone else to work with, and I would understand. Do you know what happened? Every one of these prospects became clients, and eight years later, 95 percent of them are still with me! I literally tripled my business while going through my treatments.

For me, looking for the positive and not concentrating on the negative was key to my healing. Being an entrepreneur, I wasn't sent home from a corporate job, put on sick leave, and left to dwell on what the universe was doing to me. Instead I was concentrating on helping clients, achieving great things, and spending time with my family.

During this time of treatment I was thrilled to be involved in a project that is near and dear to my heart: Women Speakers Association. The opportunity to develop and build the first version of WSA's website kept me centered. It gave me an opportunity to keep my mind fresh and be inspired by women who wanted to make a difference for other women globally. Through this process and support, many of these women have become the closest of friends, mentors, and people I just couldn't do without in my life.

I chose to rise above and embrace the "glass is half full" scenario, rather than dwell on the "what ifs." We all have to deal with roadblocks along the way—some small, some larger than life—but by focusing on what you do want versus what you don't, you can positively impact your outcome in life, business, and success.

Tracey Ehman, an online presence and social media strategist, is the go-to person for enhancing your online presence, ensuring that you not only get "found" by your target audience, but that your website and social media efforts increase your revenues. Tracey is also part of the Women Speakers Association (WSA) Executive Team, where you can find her hosting the monthly #SpeakerChats and member calls.

www.partneringinsuccess.com

STILL I RISE

From Pain to Purpose

Dr. Mary J. Huntley

We moved to the nation's capital in 1960 during a very pivotal period of the Civil Rights Movement. Dr. Martin Luther King Jr. delivered his famous "I Have a Dream" speech, emphasizing the need for jobs and freedom for Blacks during a time when racism was very prevalent. I witnessed racism repeatedly raise its ugly head denying Blacks equal compensation for work performance. Racism denied Blacks acceptance into Ivy League schools and so much more. Blacks were treated as less than human, and this caused me deep pain. I grew tired of watching the news, which depicted riots, beatings, and injustices against Blacks. I knew that there was a better way, that a positive change was necessary. Blacks deserved better education, jobs, and the same equality as other humans.

How could I make a difference? How could I empower myself to rise to the occasion when the opportunity presented itself? I knew that I needed to prepare in order to have a brighter future, especially since **proper preparation prevents poor performance**. Therefore I set **S.M.A.R.T.** goals in order to fulfill my educational quest, which would enable me to secure a well-paying job upon graduation. The first letter of the **S.M.A.R.T.** goal process is **S: Specific**. The second letter is **M: Measurable**. The third letter is **A: Attainable**. The fourth letter is **R: Realistic**. And the last letter is **T: Time-bound**.

The **S.M.A.R.T.** goal setting system will also enable *you* to achieve *your* goals in an excellent manner. Once you execute this system, you are well on the way. Remain focused! Yes, you may have some challenging moments, but remember your goal and press on until you reach it.

My specific goal was to obtain a college degree. This was a very crucial period in my life. My family was very supportive, but there was no financial support available for my college dream. I began working at a very early age to offset the cost of my back-to-school attire. I was forever cognizant to put my best foot forward on every job because I knew it was my ticket to a brighter future. I worked feverishly in the summer youth program at the D.C. Teacher's College, as a clerk-typist in President Dr. Paul Cooke's office. I received excellent ratings and continued to work in the program until I exceeded the age requirement.

I then landed a full-time job that paid my college tuition. Therefore, I worked and simultaneously attended college full-time. **This was no cake walk.** There were times when I felt like throwing in the towel, but I focused on my goal and persevered toward the finish line. I continued pressing forward in spite of challenges both at work and at home. There were many times that I resorted to positive affirmations and positive self-talk when the challenges seemed unbearable. I reminded myself that a winner never quits and a quitter never wins. It was only with God's grace and mercy and my sheer determination that I graduated with a 4.0 GPA.

Though I had achieved some educational goals, there were more goals to accomplish. Therefore I continued to work feverishly and pursue my educational quest that would lead to a brighter future. I kept working and attending classes. As I embarked upon my goal, many said that I would never accomplish it. After all, no one in my family had ever attended college, let alone received a college degree. However, I realized immediately that I could not listen to the naysayers. I kept it moving, and at the end of the day, I was able to hold my head up high, stick my chest out, and thank God that I was a winner.

I held fast to my educational goal. I kept working and attending classes. My reality was that if I wanted to complete my goal, I could not afford to be distracted by anything or anyone. I was determined to live a better lifestyle, and education was a very vital part of that process. So I persevered ahead and continued to make sacrifices. There was little time for socializing, but when I sacrificed time to visit family and friends, it was usually very refreshing. All work, study, and no play can be very dull, so I welcomed the rare occasions to socialize. Throughout my educational quest, I remained cognizant of time.

Eventually I saw light at the end of the tunnel. But it was not without what seemed to have been blood, sweat, and many, many tears. When I look back over my journey, I thank God for blessing me to accomplish my goals. The ultimate winning experience during my educational quest was when I finally earned my doctorate degree. Now I am a licensed clinical pastoral counselor with advanced certifications in Integrated Marriage and Family Therapy, Group Therapy, Cognitive Therapy, Crisis and Abuse Therapy, and Death and Grief Therapy. I am also a Board Certified Master Christian Life Coach. And I am a clinical supervisor and an international representative for a Christian Counseling Organization. To God be all the glory!

Know that you can, you must, and you will achieve your goals exercising faith in God, discipline, and determination. Presently, I spend time encouraging and empowering others (especially women) to build their lives and reach their full potential. Remember that quitting is never an option for winners. And mediocrity is not acceptable in pursuit of excellence! Always stay focused and do your part. Yes, you may get tired during your journey. You may rest during the pursuit of your goals and savor the moments, but don't quit. Always remember: "A quitter NEVER wins, and a winner NEVER quits."

Dr. Mary J. Huntley is the chief executive/ encouragement officer of Trinity Global Empowerment Ministries, Inc. She is a wife, author, prayer warrior, domestic violence awareness advocate, licensed clinical counselor, and certified master life coach. A clinical supervisor with the National Christian Counselors Association, Dr. Huntley is on a mission to empower others (especially women) to soar above the storm and reach their God-given potential.

www.drmaryjhuntley.com

HEAR MY VOICE

Dana Johnson

My voice is being heard loudly for the first time. This is the moment I have waited for my entire adult life. How do I put my experiences, advice, hopes, and feelings into words without someone judging me or labeling me? It happens daily in my industry, construction. I am either labeled a feminist or judged by the men that make up about 97 percent of the industry. Even now, in an operations-level position, the daily struggles are real.

Unfortunately, I find myself starting to become immune to a lot of the most common occurrences. Why am I having to adapt to them? "Them" meaning the thousands of men I work with and have worked with who are uncomfortable with a woman in "their space." They have almost beaten me down to the point of quitting the entire industry more than a few times, but my drive is stronger than their will to defeat me. It just took me a long time to understand and redirect my anger toward winning the fight on a larger scale versus a daily basis.

My name is Dana. I am a forty-four-year-old woman and the chief operating officer for a construction company located on the outskirts of Portland, Oregon. I am, and have always been, a single mother to my daughter, Katelynn. I grew up in Aloha, Oregon. I was a little different then most kids my age. For example, at age eleven I asked my mom for a subscription to *Money* magazine. Seriously, what kid does that? I have always been very creative and love building things. I am my father's daughter through and through: driven, logical, intelligent, with an eye for business and people.

I worked very hard when I was young and achieved a lot at a younger age than most. Usually the employees I managed were older than me. One of my previous assistants I hired and keep in touch with, Carol, is twenty years my senior. She enjoys telling the story of how she came in to the office to interview and "in comes this young girl chewing gum and twirling her hair"—she is talking about me; however, I swear I wasn't twirling my hair! She says she was thinking of running for the door until I spoke: "When Dana started talking, I was very impressed with her professionalism, poise, and intelligence." Carol was my assistant for over six years.

The experience of managing others older than me helped me later in life when I decided to work in construction. I've had a lot of pushback over the years as a manager, and even more so now. On every project I have been on, I have been pushed to many limits I know a man in my position would not have to deal with. I am constantly being quizzed or set up to have to prove my knowledge and prove that I am competent to do the job. As you can imagine, this is very trying. At a certain point, I felt like things would be easier if I started blending into my environment. So, first I stop wearing lipstick, then makeup, and then I stop doing my hair and begin wearing frumpy, loose clothing so the comments and whistles die down. I have had to do these things on every project I've been on. Again, why am I adapting?

The construction industry and other male-dominated industries can be very difficult for a woman—in any position. You discover that the team has many outings together, but you're not invited to any of them. You are excluded from the inside jokes and nicknames they laugh about in the jobsite trailer. The female typically gets stuck with the office supply order and other tasks deemed to be "secretaries' tasks," because "girls are better at that stuff"—as I have been told so many times. Every one of these situations has happened to me multiple times in the past five years. There have been times when I do break down—but only when I am alone. Only at home.

I find it interesting that the men I have talked to about these issues in construction have all said that they have never experienced this or done these things to a female. Really? They don't even see it or realize it. Only when certain instances are discussed and I break it down for them do they begin to understand. This is very frustrating. I feel like I need to draw attention to the problem, but that attention can make things worse.

It takes an extremely strong female to work in this type of position or in any male-dominated workplace. This is who I am, and this is what I am destined to do. I will be strong, stand my ground, and speak loudly to all women. My hopes and desires are clear. I want women to stand tall and proud and have their voices be heard without repercussions or other forms of discipline. I want all women to support all women—to raise each other up and empower each other. I want the new generation of men coming into construction and all industries to break the mold, change their mindset, and help other men understand the issues women face daily. I hope in the future there is a formed team of men and women who work together and earn the same wages for the same job and that no other women need to face the struggles I have.

My name is Dana, and I am speaking loudly so my voice can be heard.

Dana Johnson is the COO of a construction company in Beaverton, Oregon. She has over twenty years of high-level management experience and is a published author. She lived in Arizona for seventeen years, Silicon Valley for three years, and now is back home in Oregon. She is passionate about volunteering.

www.danaspeaks.com

THE REBEL WITHIN

Play Big in Your Own Life

Alana Love

Have you ever felt that you were living someone else's life and not your own? Have you ever felt stuck and trapped in someone else's agenda?

I believe our stories and choices determine both our relationships with life and with other human beings. Over the years, although I made choices that were great, many were poor and misdirected. Yet every choice and relationship brought me here, to sharing a little of my life and wisdom.

Choices change us or imprison us. My father was a Holocaust survivor who lost everything dear to him. Yet he chose to embrace life with fearless passion. I watched him continuously choose new experiences, and he seemed blessed with a tremendous capacity for forgiveness and love. I realized many years later that love's roots grew in the soil of his sorrow and grief. He rebelled against conformity and modeled the ability to change and flow with life. My mother was the opposite, a bruised woman tormented by mental and emotional instability, depression, and thoughts of suicide. She shut people out and retreated to make her world small and safe. It was painful to witness and experience.

As a good daughter, I was loyal to both extremes. Imitating my dad, I played passionately in my experiences, embracing opportunities for excitement and aliveness like a little child. My mother constantly reminded me this was inappropriate for a girl—that spontaneous adventures were acceptable for boys but irrelevant to my future as a lady, wife, and mother. Those two worlds collided rather harshly. I imitated my mother and started to shut down.

Desperate to feel validated and meaningful, I imitated my dad in trying to make my mother happy. That was an exercise in failure. I suppressed my enthusiasm and playfulness, and I was miserable. No matter what I said or did, it simply wasn't enough. In desperation, I chose to diminish myself and shrink down to a shadow in an effort to enter her world and make her

69

happy. And what an effort it was! The harder I tried, the more I played small. Instead of lifting her out of her misery and disappointment, I jumped into the darkness and suffered alongside her.

Many of us do that with our partners, spouse, coworkers, boss, friends, or someone we simply want to impress. We want approval and recognition. We want to feel valuable. So we compromise the beauty and greatness of our own precious uniqueness and authenticity. We remain quiet and invisible, even though Life is prodding us to speak up and show up.

The truth is, I didn't see my own worth because I wasn't living my own worth. I diminished my own value in an attempt to connect with another human being. I put someone else first and in the process misplaced my voice. As I look back, my stories are littered with invalidated fragments of myself. I failed to prove to myself that I was worthy, and so I lived quietly in pain and disappointment. I was depressed, and I hated it.

It's hard to feel valid and meaningful when you compromise your authenticity, but I was hungry to be seen and heard. I always knew there was so much more to me, but I had forgotten what my father demonstrated. If you play small to be loved, then people will think you are small. If you diminish your wisdom to be liked and stay quiet when you can change someone's life, people will think you don't have very much wisdom.

I had to learn how to boldly show up and uplift my own identity. I had to change and find a way to come alive again beyond my pain. I had to rebel against my own small stories and play bigger in my own life.

It was time to imitate the rebel nature of my father once more. I started defying the conformity that was suffocating my spirit. I took risks and crossed social boundaries. I pursued freedom and found a voice that was my own. When I fell, I fell hard. At times I felt bruised, beaten down by anguish and pain. Yet when I loved, I loved with delicious abandon. I found rules to break, and I saw how playing small is a silent killer of life's excitement and wonder.

Living takes courage. It calls for clarity, new choices, and the embracing of challenges and discomforts in order to bring celebration back into life. I've changed my story so many times, learning over and over that value doesn't come by playing small. Now I coach and train others to play larger and come alive on their own stage.

As women, we are trained to minimize our voices, be background players, and not ruffle feathers. So we hide our best. We hide the richness of our love, our spirits, and the spiciness of our contributions and wisdom. And then we struggle to find our place in life.

Our choices can lead us to an extraordinary celebration of aliveness, unity, and positive change, or they can breed a pandemic field of limitation, prejudice, judgment, and resentment where no one thrives. I know from experience the exultation of one and the weight of the other.

The truth is that so many of our stories trap us. They are familiar, even in their contractions and pain. Yet change and freedom come through the unfamiliar. I've been blessed to have unusual access to the spirit world since I was a child. It is where I've always gotten validated, and it inspired my inner rebel to come alive. And yes, Spirit yanked that rebel back from the precipice many a time!

Everything we do is a choice, and every choice leads us toward or away from a celebration of life. As a Certified High Performance Coach™ and trainer, I am grateful and inspired to witness people light up and turn on. That's all I ever wanted to see with my mother. If you can't do it with the one you want, move on to those who do want it. I do what I do because there are people in the world, men and women of incredible power, who are playing too small. That must change.

Everyone has a gift to be lived. It's time to play bigger in life. There are people waiting for you to show up as your best. Let's change what needs to be changed, and celebrate outcomes that are extraordinary, rich, and amazing.

Reach out to me at Expert Coaching Now, and let's have a conversation.

*As a higher consciousness mentor and elite Certified High Performance Coach™, **Alana Love** brings a unique mix of insight and proven systems to entrepreneurs, professionals, and individuals to virtually gain clarity, influence and strategies for success. Whether the desire is for personal or professional impact, Alana helps people choose differently, change their lives, and celebrate new outcomes. The founder of Mastery Enterprises and Expert Coaching Now, Alana currently lives in Columbus, Ohio.*

www.expertcoachingnow.com

Purpose Has Power Over Pain

Nicole S. Mason

"Nicky, Ms. Georgia is gone!"

Those were the words that rang loudly in my heart and spirit when I answered the door on November 2, 2005. My prayer partner was there to tell me that my mother had passed away in her sleep. Those words landed deeply inside of me somewhere, and it felt as though life had quickly left my body. Eight months pregnant at the time, there wasn't anything in me to hold me up, so I fell to the floor. I could hear myself screaming deep within, but no sound was heard on the outside.

My prayer partner called the paramedics. When they arrived to check me out, miraculously I was fine, the baby was fine, my blood pressure was fine. But I couldn't utter a word. I could only nod my head in agreement or disagreement. I couldn't move. I seemed to be in two places at once—my body was lying there on the floor, but my spirit had gone somewhere else. I have come to know that I was in shock. I have also come to know that shock is good; it saves our minds, and it allows time for the body and spirit to accept that which has happened that cannot be changed.

Learning to live without my mom was very difficult. I was an only child and an only grandchild. Seventeen days after my mom passed away, my grandmother passed away. I buried my immediate family in one month. I was scared, hurting deeply, unsure of my future, and experiencing all the emotions that go along with losing a loved one unexpectedly.

Although I am a woman of great faith, there were many days I did not think I was going to make it. The pain was too intense, and the reality of it all was just too overwhelming. But I had a great support system in my husband and my sister friends, and I also read everything I could get my hands on about the grieving process. I wanted to learn all I could about the sorrow I was experiencing.

I went to the mall one day, and I could not remember where I parked my car. I was overcome with fear, but later I learned that forgetting things is part of the grieving process. Another time my teeth were chattering, but I wasn't cold. It was my body's reaction to the grief that I was experiencing. One of the worst moments was when I picked the phone up to call my mom and it hit me that she wouldn't be there to pick up the phone. But God's grace and mercy helped me through the process.

I learned how to be gentle with myself and "engage the process." I engaged the process by allowing my emotions to express themselves. I didn't hold back my tears because I learned along the way that the "grief wave" was much more intense when I tried to hold it back, and it lasted longer. I realized that God knew what He was doing when He gave us the emotion of grief, and it is better to cooperate with it instead of fighting it.

Over the years since losing my mom and grandmother, I have seen how my tragedy has allowed me to help others to triumph. I have been able to console others close to me when their mothers have passed away. I have sat beside hospital beds and read Scripture, sang hymns in my best voice, and helped to usher people into eternal rest just by being there with them. I am sure that losing my own mom and grandmother strengthened me so I would be able to serve others. The day that I washed the remains of one of my dear friend's mother's body, I knew that my pain was not in vain. I understood at that very moment that my pain had purpose attached to it.

I have become a source of encouragement to many who have lost loved ones. I have come to know that God does not allow pain into our lives to punish us or to break us, although it may feel like that at the time. But God is not that kind of God. He is loving, and He allows situations in our lives to build us up so we can bless others. I am now able to let others know that they have a choice in how they honor the loved ones that have passed away. We can either be bitter or take the pain and turn it into purpose.

In addition to sitting with my friends' loved ones and holding their hands until they pass away, I have also helped to plan funerals and memorial services. I know what it's like to have to make funeral arrangements under pressure, so I have served as the voice of reason and the advocate for families in that situation. I am confident that all that I went through losing my mom and my grandmother was not just about me—it was to prepare me for how I serve others today. Psalm 119:71 sums up my experience: "It was good for me to be afflicted so that I might learn your decrees" (NIV). I can say with a holy boldness today that God is faithful, and He is a promise keeper. God has turned my mourning into dancing!

Nicole S. Mason *is a licensed attorney in the State of Maryland and the founder and CEO of Strategies For Success, LLC. In this capacity, she works with women leaders and executives to pull out what is already inside of them through the powerful practice of coaching. Nicole speaks professionally on the topics of confidence and effective leadership strategies.*

www.nicolesmason.com

THE GIFT OF BIRTHING

Reclaiming Our Power, Reclaiming Our Voice, Reclaiming Our Choice

Lakichay Nadira Muhammad

One of my beloved ancestors once made a powerful statement that I will never forget: "The hospital is not a place for a pregnant women; it is a place for those that are sick, and pregnancy is not an illness." Years later I was reminded of those words when I was blessed to witness a midwife-attended home birth. It was one of the most beautiful things I had ever seen. I knew that if God ever granted me the opportunity to be with child, I would want to recreate that same kind of magic.

By God's mercy and grace, a few years later I was blessed with the seed of life. I originally began my birthing journey aided and assisted by a wonderful and experienced midwife. But as fate would have it, I would make a decision early in my pregnancy to have a DIY birth. I knew that I wanted to experience what many of my ancestors experienced, and a healthy home birth was what I desired. Although I had no formal experience—which naturally caused a little fear to creep in—what I did have was great examples and the faith that I could deliver this gift with God's assistance.

For the next several months, I studied every book I could find relating to midwifery and natural childbirth until I became one with the knowledge I was blessed to discover. In addition I began to tap into the energy and spirit of all the great and courageous women that had gone before me. I had so many examples from many of my ancestors who had served as midwives and delivered multiple babies with no formal training to the many women around the world who had been doing this since the beginning of time.

I prided myself on being the female version of God (some may say Goddess) and knowing that I could do anything that I put my mind to. On June 14, 2000, my thoughts became flesh and I was able to see my vision manifest in the person of my firstborn son. Three years later I was blessed to repeat this magical occurrence with the birth of my second son.

The birthing process by far is one of the most fulfilling and rewarding experiences that I've been blessed with. In truth I believe that it is the closest any human being will ever come to God, because it is during these times that we must tap into our Godlike attributes. God must be present with us, guiding us every step of the way—how else does one explain such a beautiful and phenomenal experience? If you happen to be one of the many who have had this highly sacred opportunity, then you are more divinely connected than you may ever know. BIRTHING is so powerful that the entire experience should always be honored, reverenced, and highly regarded as one of the most sacred sacrifices known to man.

For the past two hundred-plus years, women in America have experienced a major shift as it relates to childbirth and the overall value of maternal health. This holistic art form that once was facilitated and assisted by skilled and experienced midwives was hijacked and corrupted by a male-dominated profession that was foreign to the art of childbirthing. Healthy babies being born in the comfort of our homes slowly became a thing of the past, while hospital births attended by doctors and nurses began to be marketed and glorified as the "new and improved" way to give birth. What happened? Who decided that this was best for women—and why? The truth of the matter is that **birthing became a business**! No longer honored and respected as a sacred experience influenced by nature, childbirth became an opportunity for the medical profession to create an additional means of income. An art form that is a natural life occurrence slowly began to be treated as a life-threatening illness that required the attention of so-called medical "experts."

Sadly, many nurses and doctors bought into the notion that women no longer deserved to have control over their maternal health. The freedom for a woman to choose how she gave birth was no longer an option, and home births and midwifery-attended births were ridiculed and looked down upon. Fear tactics scared women into thinking they were no longer safe in their homes. If they chose to have a midwife assist them in their birthing experience, somehow their babies would not get the "expert" care they needed.

Having a say in how a woman should birth her children is a God-given right. All women are born with a natural instinct to birth our babies. My experience gave me the strength to trust in myself and have the faith that ultimately afforded me the freedom to experience a God-assisted birth.

When it comes to a sacred decision centered around your birthing experience, no one should make the decision for you. Unfortunately, money and power have created a monopoly on the business of birthing. The cost to give birth in a hospital can average anywhere from $25,000 to $60,000. I am happy to say that my births were nearly 100 percent below cost.

My story is not meant to convince you about the type of birth you should have. I am here simply as an advocate for a woman's right to choose her birthing narrative without the influence or force of a history and a profession that has not always been kind or truthful regarding our maternal health, nor has always shown respect or valued the woman's divine power, sacred voice and God-given right to choose. I want to serve as an example and encourage mothers to gain more knowledge about our indigenous birthing traditions and maternal health practices around the world.

Remember, pregnancy is not an illness to be "treated"—instead, it is a natural gift from God to carry the seed of life, and it requires nurturing and care driven by love. You have options, and the role you play in your maternal health is extremely important and valuable!

Affectionately known as "The Queen of Self Improvement," AKA "The Wellness Angel," **Lakichay Nadira Muhammad** *is a wholistic health practitioner and mental health therapist who prides herself on helping clients obtain optimal health and wellness through mental, physical, spiritual, and emotional alignment. As a speaker, maternal health and parent advocate, womb wellness savant, and indigenous baby catcher, she believes that every woman is uniquely endowed with her own special gift, just waiting to be unwrapped.*

www.thecenterforselfimprovement.com

THE BEST IS YET TO COME

Donna Rae Reese

If you were told that you had only months to live, would you do things differently? Sadly, this was the reality for two of my sisters who passed away tragically within four months of each other. It certainly was an eye-opener for me as I worked through my own chronic illness.

I fell into the entrepreneur life in my early twenties, after dropping out of college and marrying very young. By age twenty-four my husband and I bought his family's pest control business. By age twenty-nine I had two sons and a second business. There was no such thing as downtime. The balance of work and home ended in an amicable divorce from my husband and business partner. We had to choose between a marriage and our businesses, and each of us relied on the business for our livelihood. We continued to work together, which was quite a process at first.

Failure was not an option. Rather than allowing myself to fall into depression, I engulfed myself in my work, raising my sons, and volunteering in my community. I was truly serving everyone's needs, while neglecting my own at times. Once my kids were grown, I purchased a third business. I also ran for a publicly elected political seat and won.

My first challenge was owning a pest control company, an industry dominated by males. Ironically, in the 1990s it was the female clients who questioned my knowledge and ability the most. Then there was the challenge of being a single mother while trying to balance a career that involved working with my ex-husband—while making sure that the life my boys were accustomed to would not change due to my sheer exhaustion and financial changes. You would have to think I was a glutton for punishment the day I decided to run for political office. But I had constantly encouraged my kids to "stand for something." I wanted to lead by example; I wanted to show my sons that getting involved and making an impact was not only needed but necessary.

There was a time when I felt completely unstoppable. I found out that this can change in an instant when I was given a medical diagnosis of degenerative disc disease. For years I battled through chronic aches and pains, chalking it up to long work hours and the stress of juggling a family and career. I did what many entrepreneurs do: I ignored the increasing warning signs because being ill did not have a time slot in my jammed daily planner. Eventually my condition turned into an emergency.

I had my first spinal fusion in 2012. Fast-forward to 2015 and five spinal surgeries later, with two neurosurgeons basically telling me that life as I knew it was over. At forty-nine years of age, I had to make the conscious decision to sell my shares of the business to my sons. Not only did I have to leave my career, but I also sought medical treatment in a warmer state because the two-and-a-half-hour commute to my doctors in the dead of winter was simply too much. Being a planner, I had done funeral preplanning, but I had never planned on being alive yet not able to live.

For two years I suffered both emotional and physical pain. The person who once was involved with everything and everyone was now alone. Many nights I prayed that I simply would not wake up to a new day. Then tragedy struck my family. My sister Jane was diagnosed with cancer and passed away in only five weeks. Four months later, my sister DeeDee died instantly from a brain aneurysm. Their tragic deaths prompted me to quit feeling sorry for myself and acted as a catalyst to find myself again. If I was alive, I was going to live! Les Brown's quote "Fear death if you want, but don't fear life" was a calling.

During the most successful time of my life, I was thriving because of my positive attitude and outlook. From my love of *The Secret*, I was a big believer in the power of a vision board. Now each day I was forcing myself to get out of bed, planting my two feet on the floor and being grateful for everything I had. I started listening again to my favorite motivational speakers, Les Brown and Grant Cardone. Charles Swindol said, "Life is 10 percent of what happens, and 90 percent of what you make of it." If my life was going to improve, my attitude needed to improve. I started loving myself again.

Doors of opportunity began opening again. I met an amazing pain management doctor who gave me hope when he introduced me to a new long-term solution. On my vision board I had put a picture of myself next to dollar signs. At the time I had no clue what the significance of that picture would become. Today it is on the cover of my book *Don't Tell Me I Can't*.

While googling career options my from my new home in Florida, my favorite motivational speaker came up in the search. The heading was "You have a story." I could literally train with Les Brown from the comfort of my own home! I didn't know if I would ever be able to work again, but I decided to delete the word *if* from my vocabulary and replace it with the word *when*.

I was finally living my life with intention again. My chronic pain was no longer going to consume me. I had overcome career bias, a divorce from a business partner, abusive relationships, moving away from my family, the death of close friends and family, as well as adversity from being involved in the political world, but I was still alive!

It's Not Over Until I Win by Les Brown has become my driving force to recreate myself for what I plan on being the best years of my life!

Donna Rae Reese is an author, speaker, coach who came from very humble beginnings. She was raised on a grape farm, the youngest of nine children. With a tenacious attitude and competitive nature, she owned her first business by age twenty-four. She showed her gratitude by volunteering in her community and was elected to a local political seat. She retired at age forty-nine and is now sharing her story of overcoming obstacles worldwide.

www.donnaraeinspires.com

A WOMAN'S SUPERPOWER

The Call For Feminine Leadership

Laura Rubinstein, CHt

I'm thirty years old, dressed in my black-and-cream power suit, ready to get some business done. **"Your power is in your softness,"** she says, looking right into my soul. I am stunned by what this highly regarded image consultant declares. This is an utter departure from my paradigm of being a strong, successful, take-charge career woman. Now my brain is stumped. How could softness be strong?

Although I want to resist, I am intrigued by this new thought and say, "Give me a softness makeover." She highlights and straightens my hair, drapes a scarf around me, and puts me in a solid-color suit. "There," she says, pleased. When I look in the mirror, I see something for the first time: a soft, approachable person. I feel vulnerable; I'm exposing a part of me that is neither on the offense or defense. Instead I am present, open, and available.

I didn't actually think this at the time, but changing how I looked on the outside was a **jumpstart to the biggest transformation of my life**.

I had to reconcile how this soft power worked on the inside. Up until that time, I was an "all business, get things done" kind of gal from New Jersey who would tell you like it is. So what would softness look like? What would it sound like, and how effectively would it work?

The journey began . . . I found myself in a workshop with a woman who proclaimed that the most powerful form of energy is feminine. Really? In the first exercise she asked, "How do you define feminine?" I wrote Laura Ashley floral print bedspreads and matching curtains, and pink flowy outfits. This description was far from my preferences. Thus, there was no way I was anywhere near being a feminine woman. This was going to be useless, futile, and my deepest fears were screaming that I would be incapable of benefiting from this information.

Nonetheless, my new mentor had an exquisite aura. I felt honored, acknowledged, and adored just being in her presence. People automatically opened doors, carried her bags, and even anticipated her needs, and she graced them all with that loving, irresistible energy. I wanted to have that effect on people! I wanted her secrets. Yet at the time I was devastated, lost without a career, and still reeling from a failed relationship.

My saving grace was **curiosity**. As a seeker, I discovered that the **secret sauce** to stepping into my power was unraveling some big misconceptions and surrendering to my essence. *Could it be that I am feminine? Is being feminine different than my preconception?* Oh yeah.

But what does being feminine have to do with being a leader or creating a successful career? And what is the connection between that and attracting and cultivating a juicy, delicious, soul-connected relationship with a lifelong partner? Everything! As I started **mapping my essential nature** onto a new paradigm of feminine energy, everything changed. I developed a new perspective of myself. My mentor encouraged me at one point to "put away the whips and chains you use on yourself." I actually had to ask her what that meant. She mentioned how critical I was of myself. To choose to **be compassionate with myself** was a new ballgame I had not considered. But it was a huge turning point.

For example, I was told that multitasking is a negative trait. Well, turns out it's a very feminine quality. I began to notice my skill at orchestrating projects, taking care of multiple responsibilities, and choosing where I put my attention.

I began to see that **the things I criticized myself for were not impeding my success when I used them with my heart's guidance and recognized their gift.** When I became **curious and compassionate** and started **making conscious choices, my superpower was unleashed.**

I wanted to embody these principles. I wrote down the golden nuggets on index cards so that at any moment I could flip through them and align with my feminine energy. These principles invited me into a softer space and guided me with their rich wisdom. I learned that **leading with my heart and implementing with my head are my power tools.** The more I practiced these principles, the more influence I seemed to garner. They worked so well that I published a deck of Feminine Power Cards containing these life and relationship enriching principles and practices.

To be successful in this new paradigm, **I had to open my heart to learn how to close business deals** in my marketing business. I stopped mimicking masculine traits as I did in the corporate world. I started trusting my intuition and softening my approach with prospects and clients alike. I gave up criticizing and instead honored and explored every emotion as vital messages from my soul that I needed to embrace, interpret, and understand. Over the years my marketing and consulting business blossomed and continues to thrive. Through this evolution, I attracted my precious divine life partner of more than thirteen blissful years. We still consider ourselves to be on our honeymoon.

The journey to feminine power is ongoing. Every day I curiously reflect upon my emotions, strive for self-compassion, and make conscious choices. As a colleague told me recently, "Laura, you're this mix of feminine energy that can direct a client without them feeling threatened. You have great strength because you are not afraid to be feminine and balance it with your masculine without acting like a man. That's impressive."

Softening my heart has attracted more clients, more business, and developed deeper relationships in my life. I've become a more effective influencer without overpowering a situation or resorting to coercion or fear-based reactions. The world can shift in an instant with conscious use of our feminine energy. I've seen it happen. We can create a peaceful planet that is safe for children, with clean air, water, and food for everyone. As we wake up to our superpower, we can take on our rightful place as the change leaders, healers, and rulers our families, communities, and the world are craving. Our feminine energy is more compelling than anything else out there. It's time for us to intentionally live, breathe, model feminine leadership, and transform our world.

Laura Rubinstein, CHt, *Social Buzz Club founder, is an award-winning social media strategist, marketing consultant, certified hypnotherapist, and best-selling author of* Social Media Myths Busted, Transform Your Body in the Mental Gym, *and* Feminine Power Cards. *She has worked with over one thousand businesses and is highly sought after for her innovative profit-generating strategies and branding work.*

www.TransformToday.com

LIFE RULES

Iva Schubart

Czechoslovakia during communism, 1982

It's a cold, miserable, gray day. It's raining and snowing at the same time. Brno is colourless. People pass each other with no sense of direction and without any expression on their faces. Humanity and joie de vivre are gone. It's almost Christmas 1982.

Jana, my "big sister," and I are going to town together. Not to buy carp, which local vessels have just delivered—the day before Christmas is still early enough to buy carp. No, right now my sister and I are focused on getting oranges. Yes, oranges!

We walk through the city with a glimmer of hope that something special is being sold somewhere. We're lucky. There is a long queue in front of a store where they sell a small range of fruit and vegetables. All the people in line are certainly not there to get regular stuff from that store. Something special is on sale today.

We both try hard to see what's being sold. But we can't figure it out from a distance. We decide to join the queue. No one seems to know what's being sold. I choose to leave the queue, asking Jana to keep my spot, and try to move to the front of the row so I can finally know what's being sold. To my surprise, I find out they are selling oranges and bananas. Extraordinary for us, for sure.

There is no choice; we might get green or brown bananas. The oranges are dry, but hey, take it or leave it. Standing in line is unpleasant. People don't talk; they just hold their position and wait for their turn. We see satisfied people with big smiles on their faces leaving with full bags of fruit. We hope that soon we also be lucky.

My toes are freezing slowly until I can't feel them anymore. I wonder whether they've already turned blue. My sister complains about the long queue; she's clearly annoyed. Expressing her impatience is not a wise thing to do, especially in these days of oppression. Fortunately, the line in front of us is getting shorter and shorter. I now have a view of the crates and boxes. Someone yells that the merchandise is almost gone. We continue to wait anyway along with everyone else.

Somebody in front of us orders a kilo of bananas. Now there might not be enough for everyone. Only two people in front of us—we are getting close! The bananas and oranges, however, are gone. Sold out. Nothing is left. We stare at the empty boxes in disbelief. I'm deeply disappointed, sad, and angry. My sister feels even worse. We walk home, with frozen feet, frustrated and outraged, and dreading the thought of facing yet another "dinner" of bread and sardines.

Life Is an Adventure

This world and its inhabitants will change. These changes are already in process. The Mayan calendar pointed to 2012 as the year when a major shift in consciousness would start to arise. As with the rebirth and transformation of our planet, we also must be able to enter a new age ready to master new challenges (climate issues, artificial intelligence, privacy issues, and so on).

There are no certainties or guarantees in this life, so don't expect them. Don't expect any bananas or oranges if there's a chance they will be sold out. It is possible, however, to set new priorities, choosing wisely and being aware that there will be multiple choices in life. Life is an adventure, a journey through time. There is no end point.

Everything is moving and changing all the time. Therefore, move through every day, week, month, and year following your inner compass. See yourself on a boat floating on the river from the fixed point of today to an unknown destination.

Live every chapter of your life to the fullest. Insert a new energy flow into your life by making choices with both your head and your heart.

What will your next chapter in life be? You create your own destination. You reach your goal by daring to embrace the unknown and live proactively at the border of your possibilities, not passively at the outer edges of your insecurities. As Stephen Covey said, "Begin with the end in mind"; focus on your goal, but achieve it by taking small steps. Be flexible and trust the ocean to be the captain of your own boat. Go with the flow, and let the waves take you to your desired destination.

The most important aspect of your life is your soul. Your age doesn't matter. You can heal the frustration and pain from the past if you choose. Be good to yourself.

As you get older, you become a better student in living your life. You learn every day so you can give more love to others. You rewrite your story daily and express gratitude for the many lessons that become your guide. The footprint you leave behind will make an even deeper imprint. This will be your heritage. Remember, the biggest wake-up call you can ever get is to actually live the life you love!

Iva Schubart *is an inspirational speaker, success coach, consultant, and author. She experienced that the Law of Attraction really exists and that it operates in every moment of our lives. She studied mechanical engineering, and after many challenges in her life, she finally found her purpose in life: to help and inspire people all over the world. Her first book,* Sanguine-Love, *is available from Amazon.*

www.ivaschubart.com

BULLETPROOF

Alicia Smith

Getting shot through the liver with an AK-47 didn't kill me. It only made me stronger, right? I would argue that Nietzsche's original statement is only partially correct. Let's say what doesn't kill you—and you work relentlessly to overcome—makes you stronger.

Life as a child was easy. My parents were honest, hardworking people. My siblings and I always had everything we needed. I lived a sheltered, comfortable life. I was raised in faith; the thread of Christianity was woven intricately into my life. My childhood gave me all the tools I would need to fulfill my dream of becoming a professional dancer. I set that goal at the ripe old age of nine. I spent every waking moment of the next nine years working on fulfilling that dream. (Do you think maybe I was a little strong-willed and determined?) After high school, as a dancer on scholarship at the University of Arizona, life was good . . . only for it to be shattered shortly after I had "arrived."

So how did I, a young, driven, small-town woman, end up in the middle of a gang fight? Why did this happen to me? How could I reach my goals now? How could this experience possibly enhance or deepen the meaning of my life? The truth is, we all go through hardships and face seemingly impossible challenges. At some point, we all ask, "Why?"

When that stray bullet found its way to me, life as I knew it came to an abrupt halt; it was gone forever. Before the shooting, I was a vibrant, independent, twenty-one-year-old woman. After the shooting, I was completely incapacitated, literally unable to lift a finger. Trauma like that doesn't just damage a person physically; it tortures you mentally, emotionally, and spiritually. It finds its way into every nook and cranny, leaving you numb, helpless, and dead inside.

My wounds were horrendous; countless complications arose. I had a hole the size of a man's fist in my skeletal body. After fifteen abdominal surgeries, I had deep, dark circles under my lifeless eyes. My hair was falling out. I could not walk on my own. My heart was broken. My spirit was close behind. I mourned the life I had lost.

Drowning in my own sorrow and self-pity, I was at my lowest point. Each day hatred for the man who had done this to me grew and penetrated deeper into my soul. The darkness had a death grip on me. I had no hope. The events of that night had led me to become resentful of any and everything that crossed my path.

After endless soul-searching, I came to realize that I had a choice in all of this. I could not control what had happened or even what was going to happen. I could only control how I responded. My choice was quite simple. This was either going to make me bitter or better. We all have that choice. No matter what is taken, no one can take that away!

After that life-altering revelation, an emotional healing process began. I wrestled with the loss of the life I used to live, moving through anger, depression, and finally acceptance. Piece by piece I was being restored. Unfortunately, none of it mattered if I couldn't let go of what had happened.

It took me years to realize that forgiving the person who shot me didn't diminish what happened. It wasn't an acknowledgment that what the perpetrator did was acceptable. His reprehensible and thoughtless actions showed a complete disregard for human life; he couldn't care less about me. Yet I was the only one continuously being damaged by my resentment and hate. My lack of forgiveness continued to devastate me but didn't touch him. Forgiveness would allow me to let go of the anger that was encapsulating me. Forgiving my assailant would allow me to be free.

I was able to find peace and forgiveness in the most unusual way, in the most extraordinary circumstances. It was a moment that swept me clean, a moment that would change the trajectory of my life.

Life is hard. We tend to avoid and try to escape our difficulties. Instead, we must attempt to face our trials with courage. Not an easy task, I might add. Nevertheless, it allows us to seek the opportunity to grow because adversity can always be a catalyst for growth. Who wants to be who they were ten years ago? Not me. Of course, growth takes perseverance and faith. Forgiveness? Forgiving requires strength—I believe from a power bigger than yourself.

My decision to vanquish my suffering transformed me. I learned that my inner attitude didn't have to reflect my outward circumstances. My life is not what I had expected, but whose is? That initial gunshot wound left me with less than a 1 percent chance of survival, but I didn't just survive—I fought, overcame, and thrived. I will never set aside the moments in life that have changed who I am. Neither should any of you. We all experience times in life that seem to destroy our lives and make us question everything we have ever believed. But we can't just fall victim to the circumstances life has handed us. We must rise about them.

Now my life is what I have chosen to make it. I still have dance, although it's very different from the aspirations of my youth. I have an amazing family, a devoted husband, and four children, including a miracle baby. All this has been afforded to me through the very circumstances I thought destroyed my life.

Furthermore, I now have a voice—a voice to speak on behalf of those who do not get the opportunity to speak for themselves due to violence. Most importantly, it is a voice to share my journey down the path of destruction and despair to peace, joy, and hope.

I guess what doesn't kill you *will* make you stronger . . . if you allow it to. It's in those times of tragedy that you can use what is perhaps one of the most powerful tools you have as a human: the will to live. To live and to triumph!

Alicia Smith is an inspirational speaker, author, dance and music teacher, wife, and mother. She works to help others that have faced tragedy by speaking and sharing her personal story of survival and accomplishment after being shot with an AK-47. Alicia believes that adversity can always be a catalyst for growth. You can read the full story of Alicia's struggle in her autobiography Thread.

www.aliciasmithspeaks.com

Being Me

Corinna Stoeffl

"Who am I?" is a question I used to ask a lot in my adult life. No matter the individual stories of our lives, most of us grew up with the projections of our parents, members of our extended family, teachers, family friends—you get the picture—about who we are and how we are supposed to be. However we dealt with them, they had a major impact in forming who we are today as individuals, how we see ourselves, and what our lives are like.

As a result, was I actually able to enjoy *my* life, or did I live the life others told me I should have? I was really good at the latter. I "knew" who I was supposed to be as a wife, a mother, and a daughter. At the same time, there was a restlessness in me; I was dissatisfied. I was very clear that I did not want to be the kind of mother I had experienced. I wanted more—more for myself and more for my kids. I vividly remember hearing the negative language of my mother come out of my mouth, and at that moment I decided to change. Years later, as an adult, my daughter told me how initially unsettling that change was for her since it was so fast. Looking back from today's perspective, I know I made an incredible demand of myself to be *me* and not imitate someone else.

I also used to be very serious. This seriousness covered up a level of sadness that today I would call depression. Yet I liked to laugh; I even trained myself to laugh soundlessly since laughter was not appreciated when growing up. There was such a sense of being wrong, no matter what. I didn't know enough; I wasn't smart enough; I had no self-esteem. I based my reality on how others saw me.

Did I have a sense of what was really true for me? Did I know what I would like my life to be like? No—not even in my fifties. I had been so trained to consider the needs of others first that I had absolutely no clue what I liked. I finally chose to go on the adventure of finding out what I liked. That meant that at times I had to experience something and find out I did not like it in order to get to what I did like.

I began to connect with people who saw me differently: as smart, kind, curious, capable, even potent. Very slowly my self-image began to change. I began to have experiences where I knew, where I was aware, where I perceived things around me. As a result, I changed, and as my kids were getting ready to leave home, I implemented those changes. I began to live life on my terms. The rebel in me grew ever stronger, and I started to choose what worked for me.

Imagine waking up in the morning with a sense of gratitude, feeling good about yourself, not needing to continuously prove anything to others. Today I have a much stronger sense of who I really am, and I'm free of others' projections. Knowing what is true for me allows me to choose what makes it fun for me to live. I have stepped into a level of freedom and awareness that permits me to continuously ask questions and create my life. Today, I am not just alive—I really enjoy my life. Every day is an adventure now that I am willing to be present with what is and not hide behind a pretense.

Being me is not about succeeding as the person I decided I am. It is about the energy of me, whatever that may be. When I got to the point of really being myself, I stopped being at the mercy of the world around me. I no longer felt the need to create a predictable life or be in control of everything. That had required a ton of energy and way too much judgment in order to decide if I was doing the right thing. There was very little space in my life to just have fun due to the constant referencing I had to do. That way of life no longer worked for me, and I chose to "be me."

Today I am choosing a new adventure in "being me"—letting go of the definitions I have of myself and stepping into an even greater level of freedom and choice. Instead of defining myself, I now create myself anew every day, every moment. When I stop trying to define myself, self-judgment falls away. Without definition, there is no longer a right or wrong; there is no judgment at all. What if "being me" could lead to liking myself so much that it no longer matters what others think of me, including what I think of myself!

What if "being me" is no longer following conventions, not from a rebellious point of view, but a pragmatic one. For me the continuous question is what will create more, not just for me but for all. In the moment, it still matters what I think of myself, and, at the same time, I can perceive the possibility of it ceasing to matter. "Being me" is a huge gift I've given myself. It is also a gift to others, as I invite them to be who they are. "Being you" is available to everyone who chooses it, at no matter what age. There can be ease and greatness in our lives, no matter what!

*For most of her life, **Corinna Stoeffl** searched for the answer to "Who am I?" Today she is a Certified "Being You" Facilitator with Access Consciousness®. She coaches individuals and groups, teaches courses, and gives presentations.*

www.beinginawareness.com

MINDSET MATTERS

Lessons I Wished I Had Learned Earlier in Life

Kimberly Sulfridge

Do you ever wonder why some people are more successful than others? Why do some seem to have it all together, while others struggle just to get by? Is it luck? Do they know the right people? Are they in the right place at the right time?

Actually, the only kind of luck out there is the kind we make. Knowing the right people and being in the right place at the right time are situations we create by surrounding ourselves with like-minded individuals and getting involved in our passions. What I have come to realize over time is that our brain is the most powerful tool we possess and our actions have far-reaching effects. How we respond to situations and what we tell ourselves can either make or break us. We learn many lessons throughout our lives, but there are a few that can really make a difference in how we live.

Embrace the "F" Words: fear and failure. Fear is an interesting emotion, one we all possess. While it is often healthy, such as fearing a wild animal, it can also be debilitating and stop you from moving forward. Take the fear of failure. That's a fear most of us can understand. No one likes to fail, myself included. When I was younger, if I didn't know ahead of time that I would be successful, I wouldn't even try. It saddens me to think of everything I may have missed by not trying just because I was afraid to fail. I finally came to realize that failure is a vital step that should not be skipped. Failure is only failure if you make a choice to quit. However, if you make the decision to analyze your mistakes and adjust, that failure will become a success. The important thing to remember is that as you keep trying, keep pushing forward, and keep making adjustments, success will happen. Treat failure as a learning opportunity. Whatever it is you are working toward will be the stronger for it.

Always have a goal. It's important always to have something to reach for. I learned this lesson the hard way. I was a competitive athlete growing up, and my goal was to earn a spot on the US Olympic Tennis Team in the 1992 Summer Olympics. An unfortunate accident brought that dream to a halt when I was fifteen. Doctors told me I would never play competitive sports again, and I was looking at a long and agonizing rehab. However, with a determined physical therapist and a new goal, I set out on my way. It was not easy and indeed not a success-only journey, but two years later I re-qualified for the championship level in the state of Texas. However, my victory was short-lived. I couldn't seem to win a match after that. I was playing just fine, but something was missing. It took me years to figure it out, but finally I realized I had lost "drive." I hadn't set another goal. I wasn't playing poorly; I just didn't have a finish line to reach for. It may have taken me some time to realize it then, but I promise you I will never forget this lesson.

Find your tribe. You hear the phrase "find your tribe" a lot these days. I want to change it a bit and suggest making "tribe" plural. Most of us have more than one tribe—we have friends, family, church, work, and so on. All of them are very important. I'm suggesting that we take it up a notch in all aspects of our lives, both personal and professional. I found my business tribe a few years ago. I have been a serial entrepreneur for most of my life. However, in 2015 I came across the concept of masterminds. This idea has been around for hundreds of years, yet I was just learning about it. A mastermind is a small group of like-minded individuals that get together on a regular basis to collaborate, work through challenges, bounce ideas back and forth, and generally hold one another accountable. What a concept! All this time I had been going it alone in my businesses, trying to work out every issue myself, big or small. I'm an intelligent person, but I don't know everything. How could I? We all have strengths and weaknesses. Why not work together to make everyone stronger? It's such a simple idea, yet one with so much impact.

Practice forgiveness. This is a difficult concept for many of us, mostly because we might not understand what forgiveness really means. Many of us feel that forgiving someone means we are letting them off the hook and saying that whatever they did is okay. That is not at all what it means to grant forgiveness. In actuality, forgiveness is more about the person doing the forgiving than the offender. This can be difficult for most of us to accept because we want the offender to acknowledge and take responsibility for what they have done. The problem is that may never happen.

A few years ago my father passed away, and I suddenly found myself the owner of his adventure company. I had owned and operated many companies at this point, so I was not overly concerned. However, I ran into a dynamic I was not expecting—a senior employee had a real issue with female authority. It created much unnecessary stress in an already stressful situation. It took time, as well as a significant toll on me, but I was able to resolve the issue eventually. Sometime later I was able to finally put it all behind me and forgive the employee. It wasn't easy, but I had come to realize that it was hurting me to stay angry. It was time for me to start taking care of myself, and I had to let it go in order to do that.

Your mindset is the key to the life you want to live. Successful people keep a healthy mindset even when the going gets tough. If you don't like your path, change it. Take control. No one ever said life was going to be easy or even fair. We are all dealt a different hand—some certainly better than others—but that doesn't mean we have to stay where we are. The only thing that matters is what you do right now. Make sure you have something you are reaching for. Let go of the baggage and all the negative energy that only holds you back. Find those who will lift you up and challenge you. Don't waste your life giving your power away to others. Your mindset makes all the difference in the world!

Kimberly Sulfridge is a serial entrepreneur, facilitator, author, speaker, traveler, photographer, sports enthusiast, wife, and mother of two adorable fur babies. She creates and facilitates mastermind groups for small business owners and speaks on entrepreneurship and teaching kids about money. She believes the right mindset is all the luck you need.

www.kimberlysulfridge.com

LifExtension In 3

A Mom's Journey to a Successful and Purposeful Life

Dr. Lina Thakar

In June 2004 I boarded a plane for the first time in my life. I was heading to the United States permanently, completely broken on the inside and leaving my twelve-year-old son behind. I panicked as the plane doors closed and told the flight attendant that I wanted to get off the plane. With a heavy heart I left India, where I had been born and raised, not knowing if I would ever see my son again. No, this is not an immigrant's story; it's the story of a mom who decided to change the condition of her life.

At age two I became septic when I was bitten by a tick while playing in the water. Every modern medicine approach was applied and failed, and the doctors were ready to give up. One day they told my parents to gather all the relatives together as I would die that night. My parents instead decided to embrace an unconventional path and immediately moved me to a farm as a last resort. With organic food and soil, I was back on my feet in just two weeks.

Inspired by this, by age five I had decided to become a healer. I became a very special kind of doctor, a doctor of Ayurveda medicine. This holistic healing system allows your body to heal itself in a non-pharmaceutical way. Having literally avoided a death sentence myself, I felt I was on borrowed time, and I had no choice but to offer this proven natural healing process to others.

Soon I became very successful. Life was more than perfect—I had a wonderful son (being a mom is still the best role in my life)—and then everything collapsed like a house of cards. Unfortunately, my marriage was struggling. I decided to change the conditions of my life. Being a woman, I was questioned, and everyone turned their back on me. Even my father disowned me.

And so, not knowing where I was going, I left my son with my (now) ex-husband and boarded that plane, thinking I had lost everything, possibly even my work. I did not even speak English, but to my amazement, just two months later, I got a call asking if I could offer my services as an Ayurveda doctor. People began approaching me for integrative health solutions. Soon I found myself busy helping people reverse their chronic sickness, regain hope, feel increased energy, and re-engage in life with my expertise and offerings. People consulted with me from all over the country; some even flew to Pittsburgh (where I had settled) to seek my help. To meet this growing need, I created an integrative wellness and healing program.

I simplified my life-extension process into three easy steps that potentially can eliminate or reverse chronic sickness, fatigue, and pain. These three steps are: REACTIVATE, REVERSE, and RESTORE. I call my program LifExtenstion In 3, and it's designed to assist my clients to live longer by redesigning their health.

Step 1—REACTIVATE: First, it is important to reactivate your own inner healing power by simply improving your digestion. When your digestion is struggling, the best organic foods, grass-fed meats, and even probiotics may not be absorbed, and thus the investment you're making for better health goes to waste. Simple healing foods may improve the status of your digestion, allowing for healing and the absorption of nutrients that may result in improved energy.

Step 2—REVERSE: The main reason people contact me is that they feel stuck being on multiple medications, the conventional path seems to only manage their symptoms, and they often feel fatigued and confused. The truth is that their internal toxins are blocking any healing; hence a nurturing detox process becomes important to rewire their inner physiology. It may be allergens, or even chemical toxins or emotional toxins such as suppressed anger, abuse, or trauma. When these toxins are released from the body, not only are symptoms reduced, but it may set the path to reverse the sickness. This REVERSE process is a very important step for lifExtenstion.

Step 3—RESTORE: After reactivating the healing power within and establishing a reversing path to achieve balance, we apply the restore process by using mental and spiritual practices along with healing herbs (which are simple foods). This establishes profound health restoration.

These three steps are a proven process to redesign your health. I have helped over ten thousand clients during the past twenty-five years through the LifExtenstion In 3 program. It is important to take care of your health first, so you can be with your family more, support your loved ones by being there longer, and be productive for financial growth if that is your goal. We all have limited time here on earth, and this healing path may reverse the aging process.

Today I celebrate twenty-five years of my Ayurveda Integrative Wellness practice. And yes, my son soon joined me in USA. I am very thankful to my clients who put their trust in me and have enjoyed reversal from chronic sickness, fatigue, and pain.

I am very grateful to America for giving me a new and purposeful life as an Ayurveda doctor, healer, and wellness mentor. America gave me my life back, along with my self-esteem. Now my only wish is to offer my LifExtenstion In 3 programs to empower people by regaining health. As a professional speaker, I'm also able to spread my message to the larger community. If you are struggling with imbalance or chronic sickness and feel stuck with the conventional path, or if your doctors have given up on you, you may explore an unconventional solution to be healed naturally and potentially live longer by redesigning your health.

Dr. Lina Thakar is an internationally recognized Ayurveda doctor, wellness mentor, professional speaker, and author. She has helped over ten thousand clients to achieve balanced health over her 25 years of successful practice. As a holistic doctor and a professional speaker, her key vision is to spread the message to help people redesign their health by natural ways so they can potentially live longer.

www.drlinathakar.com

CHANGE YOUR SELF-IMAGE
AND SUCCEED

Romance Waddington

I was born in Zambia, one of thirteen children. My first traumatic experience happened when I was three years old. My parents divorced, and shortly afterward I had a new stepmother. At the age of six, my great-grandmother died. I was devastated because I was her favorite. I was given the nickname "Grandma's Handbag" because wherever she went, you could be sure to find me. Then, at age seven, my mother died. I didn't get any counseling, therapy, or even any hugs when these incidences occurred. Neither did my brothers and sisters. We were just expected to get on with it.

We never talked about my mother in our house; it was as if she had never existed. I knew next to nothing about her—what she loved, what she hated. I had no idea what her favorite foods, songs, or colors were. I longed to know what her dreams and hopes for herself and her children had been.

In the meantime, with that safety net gone, my stepmother used her tongue as a weapon. She said the most horrific things—terrible things to say to a small child—as my dad stood by and let her get away with it. In fact, none of the adults around us ever held her accountable; instead they ingratiated themselves to her because my dad had money and they wanted to be a part of the good life.

As a teenager, I started writing songs about stopping corruption, saving the children, living in a world where love was the main thing and hatred was banished forever. I wanted to be somebody, to amount to something, and my dreams of becoming a world-famous singer were born.

As I grew older, though, I became my own worst critic. Whenever I did something good and felt good about myself, I would immediately be filled with guilt or shame for feeling happy. I would then analyze myself and pick holes in my behavior. When I started singing on stage, I would remember my stepmother's words—"You can't sing; you are a terrible singer. You sound like a woodpecker!"—and I would come off stage and critique myself so badly that eventually I stopped singing altogether. I still wrote songs, though, because expressing myself this way was cathartic.

I felt insignificant both in my family and in the world. I didn't really have friends, either. Most of my school friends got to see each other on the weekends, but we weren't allowed to go out on the weekends, so I mostly saw my friends at school. I developed acute panic attacks, and over the years they worsened, and I even contemplated ending it all. When I had children of my own, my children kept me alive because the thought that they might go through what I went through pulled me back from the brink every single time.

When I reached age forty, I became depressed, and my hair started to fall out. I remember thinking, *Is this it? Is this what my life is all about? Where was the young girl who wanted to change the world, kick down doors to stop corruption, and save the children of the world?* I thought, *It's too late now; I guess I can't be, do, or have what I want in life.*

I asked myself questions like *Why am I here? What is my purpose in life? What is my life all about?* I asked these questions every night. The answers didn't come right away. But when they did, I was ready to listen.

Life has a way of answering our questions, and that's why it's important to ask the right questions. I didn't know this at the time, but now I know better. I always ask myself the right questions rather than ones whose answers would be detrimental to my well-being. I was introduced to a book called *The Power of Your Subconscious Mind* by Dr. Joseph Murphy. A whole new world opened up to me! My whole body resonated with what I was reading. I was ready! In all of my forty years, I had never read anything like it, but I knew it was the truth and I knew my life would never be the same again. As Ralph Waldo Emerson said: "The mind, once stretched by a new idea, never returns to its original dimensions."

From this I came across books by Bob Proctor, Lisa Nichols, Les Brown, Jack Canfield, James Allen, Ralph Waldo Emerson, Abraham Hicks, Napoleon Hill, Earl Nightingale, and finally my mentor and go-to teacher, Neville Goddard. In these teachings I heard something that changed my life: *thoughts become things*. All teachers throughout the ages have said this in various forms. I began to study this earnestly.

Next I came across a book called *Psychocybernetics* by Dr. Maxwell Maltz, a plastic surgeon who treated people with scars or facial disfigurements. He found that some people were able to thrive and become successful after the operations, whereas most couldn't get past how they saw themselves due to having a negative self-image. He described self-image as a mental blueprint or picture of ourselves that we carry within us, and this controls what we can and cannot accomplish or what is difficult or easy for us. It is our own conception of the "sort of person I am." This helped me realize that I had a self-image of someone to whom life happened, someone who was weak and powerless to do anything to change her circumstances.

I also learned that I could change and modify my self-image and become successful in all areas of my life. This helped me turn my life around, and now I help others turn their lives around too. I constantly remind myself of how strong, wonderful, and successful I am, and I truly see myself as such.

Romance Waddington is a self-image mastery expert, motivational speaker, life coach, author, singer/songwriter, and serial entrepreneur. She has given talks on self-image at business networking events, in schools, at Rotary meetings, as well as open forums. In her spare time Romance is a keen amateur gardener who loves to explore the connections between the earthly garden and the mind. She is married with four children and lives in Derbyshire, England.

www.romancewaddington.com

CHANGES AND CHOICES

There Is Life After Divorce

Fran Watson

Our lives change at a rapid pace. The time seems to fly by, and we wonder where it has gone. How did we get to be as old as we are when we still feel so young inside? How did the children we once looked after grow up to be parents? How did our families grow and change so quickly? So many changes! We are exposed to more and more changes every day. Sometimes we may want to just scream, "Stop the world and let me off. I want to rest for a while."

The pain in my chest was so intense, I wondered if I would survive. It seemed like my heart was puffing up, expanding at a tremendous rate, and I thought it would explode right through my chest. It was almost unbearable. The tears fell in torrents as I gasped for breath.

My marriage had ended. I had asked him to leave. I finally had tired of his affairs and knew I could make it on my own. But the hurt and raw emotion of the past twenty years seethed through my body and threatened to burst through its very cells. His leaving felt like it wrenched the heart right out of my body, leaving me nothing but pain and emptiness. Now I had to make a decision. What would I do? I was determined to give my four children the best life I could. The decision I made was twofold. One was to begin my university degree, and the other was to devote my life to raising my children the best way I knew how.

A married woman becomes a single woman for one of two reasons: death or divorce. When a woman loses her husband to death, the neighbors all rally around her and provide meals and any help they can give, from household repairs and cleaning to anything else she might need. They are willing to provide comfort and a shoulder to cry on. They include her in their activities, feeling sorry for her that she is now so alone.

However, things are quite different when a marriage ends due to a marital breakdown. That immediately plunges a woman into a new category. I was transformed, instantaneously it seemed, from a married woman to a divorcee. I became part of a group of used and discarded women, seen as suspect by all those who are still safely ensconced in the womb of their marriages.

People withdrew from me. Invitations to get-togethers ceased. Thinking their husbands might be attracted to the idea of an "available woman," women who used to be my friends disappeared and left me alone with my tears and fears. There were no meals prepared and no offers of help. Husbands were kept at home just in case. The husbands might not be safe; I might cause the destruction of other marriages.

And so, in place of invitations to parties or neighborhood barbeques, there was now an empty mailbox, and the phone stayed quiet. I checked it every now and then to make sure it was still working. I began to feel as though I no longer existed; it was as if, because I was no longer half of a relationship, I ceased to be a part of the neighborhood. My children were no longer invited to play with the neighbors' children.

I came to realize that life is what you make of it. It's not about what happens "out there." Too many people waste time blaming others for what goes on in their life instead of taking responsibility for their own actions. Life is full of "if onlys." I decided that I could spend my time thinking about my broken heart, or I could pick up the pieces and move on. I worked full-time and studied at night after the kids were in bed for thirteen years, achieving my degree in 2000 at the age of fifty-one.

We all have choices to make in our lives. Some choices we make turn out well and some don't, but the choices are ours alone to make, and that is the thing we need to remember. It's a waste of time to lay the blame on something or someone outside of ourselves. It's up to us how we choose to live.

Choices
You can do and you can be
whatever you want.
You have the power
and the right
to make the changes.

There are changes to be made
as daily life goes by.

There are changes in our world
and changes in our lives.
There are those who come
and those who go.
There are those who enrich,
and those who drain.
There are thoughts
which improve our daily grind,
and there are thoughts
that depress us and bring us down.

Every chance meeting,
every friendship,
every love,
changes us inside and out
in ways we neither see
nor notice
until sometime later.
All of a sudden we encounter
an old circumstance
but we handle it in a new way
a better way.
The changes have caused us to grow,
to improve
and we can move on
unafraid.

For over thirty years **Fran Watson** *has developed and facilitated various workshops. She obtained her degree at the age of fifty-one doing correspondence courses and working full-time while raising her four children. Fran is a firm believer in personal growth, serving on the executive of Toastmasters clubs and mentoring others in public speaking and career decision-making.*

www.simplestepstospeakingsuccess.com

No More Unhappy Endings

Dr. Bria White

Just stop! Don't fight so hard to breathe. Just close your eyes and it will all be over soon. Face it . . . this is how you die. My inner voice drowned out the raging animal-like sounds of my attacker. A moment of calm—it felt so appealing to just let go of life. Logic told me that the steady pressure being applied to my neck would eventually kill me. My body ached all over. I wasn't yet fully aware of the trauma to my head, the injury to my spine, and the un-speakable damage to my soul. I just knew that I wanted it all to end. I just wanted the bad man to stop!

How could this be happening to me? I had followed all the rules to deserve my "happier-ever-after life." After all, I was a former beauty queen, and I had earned a college degree. All my children were born in wedlock. And I had chosen the noble career of a Christian educator. My husband was a US Army veteran with a secure IT career. We were seen as pillars of the com-munity—the picture of perfection! We seemingly had it all: the big house, the fancy cars, the perfect children. To the outside world, our life story read like a fairy tale. But within those majestic walls, we hid an insidious secret.

What will become of my children? The thought struck me like the shock of a heart defibrillator. Just like that, self-pity vanished, and I regained the will to live. He must have sensed the change in my resolve because he released his hold on me. Laughing, he smirked, "Are we having fun yet?"

He answered his own question. "Yes, I think we should have some wine now." Unable to stand, dazed by the blows to my head, I decided that my best chance for survival was "to play nice." So for the next forty-eight hours, I complied with all his demands, downplayed my injuries, and assured him that all would be forgiven. All the while, I chose my words carefully, mon-itored his moods, and plotted my exit strategy.

Monday morning arrived, and it just happened to be payday. Led by his greed, he struggled with the idea of releasing me just long enough to get that check. Eventually he confronted me with clear instructions to pick up my check, fake an illness, and come straight back home. I had just endured two-and-a-half days of sleep deprivation and abuse: verbal, emotional, physical, and sexual. Frankly, I was too exhausted to fight anymore. So I lovingly agreed to comply. To my surprise, he handed me my purse and kissed me on the cheek, releasing me into the early morning light. I struggled to appear humble, hide my injuries, and contain my jubilation.

And yes, I followed his directions step-by-step. I got in my car, went to work, picked up my check, faked an illness, and left. But I never went home again! Like a scared animal, I sat in the parking lot of the bank, cash in hand, my heart racing, and my mind wondering, *What's next? What do I do now? Where do I go? More importantly, Where will I be safe?* You see, even after all those years of formal education, no one had ever prepared me for the day when I would have to escape my *knight in shining armor*, my best friend, my husband, and ultimately my abuser. I didn't have a safety plan. I just knew that I could not return to that house, to that false narrative, to that superficial life. I had passed the point of no return. I left all my precious belongings behind. I started my journey toward freedom with just my car and my purse.

It was unbelievable that I had ignored all the warning signs of an abusive relationship and held on to the fantasy that everything would work itself out. I constantly reminded myself that every marriage had "good times and bad times." Perhaps I was just "too emotional," as my abuser often claimed. After all, the most important thing was to keep the family together . . . for the sake of the children. My religious beliefs offered endless stories of the rewards of being "long-suffering." I had often dreamed of our fiftieth anniversary when I would be proud that "our love had stood the test of time." In the name of love, I had given up my most basic rights as a person. I had armed myself with all the clichés about "true love" instead of the truth. I had lost myself and disconnected from my feelings, needs, wants, and desires. I normalized and justified the chaos and turmoil as the price that a "good wife" pays for the "perfect life."

Truthfully, no woman ever expects to be in an abusive relationship. Yet, Domestic Violence (DV) is a problem that affects every community across the country. It crosses all races, social and economic backgrounds, cultures, religions, and relationship types. Perhaps the answer lies in the famous fable about how a frog put in tepid water which is then slowly brought to a boil will not perceive the danger until it is cooked to death.

It has been over a decade since I fled for my safety. Despite all I have been through, I am happy, healthy, and wiser. I am committed to living more fully. As a DV survivor, speaker, and activist, I have turned my experience into a teachable moment by launching a teen program entitled "Like Shopping for Shoes." Without education, dating violence and domestic violence are rapidly becoming a reality for too many. Upon reflection, I wish that I had been educated about the rights and responsibilities of relationships—or at least taught something about setting boundaries, personal space, intimidation rituals, and deal breakers. Frankly, I wish that someone had said something, done something, or taught me something about this social issue before that near fatal event.

Now that you have heard my story, I encourage you to do something! Join me in the national conversation about DV, teen-dating violence, and relationship rights. Lend your support to the grassroot efforts of #metoo, #timesup, or #nomore! Doesn't everyone's story deserve a happy ending?

Dr. Bria White, *author, speaker, and activist, is thoroughly entertaining and delightfully funny with a brutally honest delivery style that touches the heart of every listener. She has been called an "inspiration," a "realist," and a "true leader" for her resiliency to life's most challenging experiences. The author of* The Official Parent Handbook: Spare the Rule, Spoil the Child, *Dr. White also speaks regularly and writes for several blogs and magazines.*

www.drbriawhite.com

It's Time for Your Voice to Be Heard!

As women step up as leaders in every industry, on every continent, Women Speakers Association is here to support you to feel empowered to speak from any stage, whether it be directing a boardroom, hosting a webinar, leading a session at the UN, etc.; to use your voice to guide, inspire, educate, train, and motivate.

With over thirty years' experience behind the scenes in the speaking industry, we know how challenging it can be to position yourself powerfully as a woman in order to get your message out and make the difference you came here to make.

We're Here to Help Grow Your Visibility So You Get Seen, Booked, and Paid!

We are here to provide solutions to the issues you tell us are most important to you, whether that's getting booked on the big stages, growing your visibility, promoting your events and products, or bringing you a sense of community when you feel like you're out there going it alone.

Be Part of the First-Ever Global Gathering Place for Women Speakers in Over 120 Countries

We invite you to join us in this collaborative, conscious "movement," a growing sisterhood reaching women in 120 countries on six continents transforming how you get yourself and your message out into the world. We're here to help you positively impact the lives of your clients, your companies, your communities, and the world.

WSA WOMEN SPEAKERS ASSOCIATION

www.WomenSpeakersAssociation.com